PARENTING WITH PROVERBS:

A Workbook For Families

Richard S. Hockett

Copyright © 2013 by Richard S. Hockett

Parenting with Proverbs
by Richard S. Hockett

Printed in the United States of America

ISBN 9781626977143

All rights reserved solely by the author. The author guarantees all contents are original and do not infringe upon the legal rights of any other person or work. No part of this book may be reproduced in any form without the permission of the author. The views expressed in this book are not necessarily those of the publisher.

Unless otherwise indicated, Bible quotations are taken from the New International Version. Copyright © 1984 by International Bible Society.

www.xulonpress.com

This family workbook
is dedicated to
my children,
Rich and Rachel,
for whom it was first written in 1980.

Preface for Fathers

This workbook on Proverbs is to help fathers teach their families the practical wisdom of God. The charge to teach your children and wife wisdom is primarily to you, the father, not the church, Sunday School or Christian school (Ephesians 6:4; 1 Corinthians 14:35; Ephesians 5:25-27).

Some fathers may believe they are too busy to teach their families the practical wisdom of God. But David, when he was King of Israel, taught his son Solomon when he was "still tender" the importance of wisdom (Proverbs 4:3-9). Later when Solomon became King of Israel, he asked the Lord in a dream for a discerning heart to govern God's people. The Lord gave Solomon a wise and discerning heart (1 Kings 3:5-12) that exceeded all others. Solomon asked for discernment instead of riches and honor because of what his father had taught him. I doubt that any of us fathers are busier than David was.

Some fathers may believe they are too imperfect to teach their families the practical wisdom of God. But David, when he taught his son Solomon the importance of wisdom, was both an adulterer and a murderer. In fact, David's sins were the basis of Psalms 51 and 32; these were worship songs! Imagine Solomon as a child hearing these songs about his father. I doubt that you are more imperfect than David was, and David taught his son Solomon the importance of wisdom. God's wisdom is greater than our faults as fathers!

On a personal note regarding myself as a distant and imperfect father, I got caught up in a fast track career in a Fortune 500 company and then realized when I was 35 years that I was living a separate life from my wife and children. I made a career change in order to reconnect with my family, and then wrote and taught this workbook as part of my reconnecting and fulfilling my responsibilities to my family. This was one of the best decisions I ever made.

Your family should find the various topics very relevant to their daily lives. Many of the issues discussed—money, friends, diligence, response to aggression, discipline, etc. – are going to arise sooner or later anyway. These lessons will provide an opportunity for you to lay a foundation of proper values and guidelines for your family.

The discussion times should be a valuable tool for stimulating communication and understanding between family members. Make them relaxing and enjoyable.

The challenge for you as the teacher is not to master the content of this workbook so that you might instruct your family. The challenge is for you to respond to the correction of Proverbs first, to be a model of wise response. The key is not for you to know all the answers or show yourself perfect, but for you to show a true desire to see God change your imperfections. Sharing your failures to match up to God's wisdom, and your desire to change will open the way for your family to respond in a genuine way. Such a father leads his family in the practice of seeing God become strong where we are weak (our failures).

The following format worked for us, but other formats may be used in your particular situation. Each member does the lesson separately, unless the younger children need help with word meanings or understanding the questions. Fathers, I implore you to complete each lesson yourself. Having gone through this workbook with my own family, I knew the temptation to "let them do the work; I'm too busy." Don't give in.

Our family made a commitment to take several weeks in late summer to go through the workbook on a daily basis. We had seen the wisdom of Proverbs work in our lives before, so this commitment came easily. We expected God to bless bountifully. He did. During the school year, a schedule of one to two lessons per week might be more doable and still involve a high degree of commitment in the middle of our hectic family lives.

Some time should be set aside for family members to prepare, followed by a time of discussion. During the discussion, each family member could share a verse from the assigned chapter of Proverbs and explain what it meant to them or why they liked it. The family can then recite the memory work together if they are doing the optional memorization.

The father should then read the lesson introduction and address the questions among the family, giving all a chance to participate. Some questions are designed for personal sharing and each person should respond to these.

Openness in sharing will be determined by how openly you yourself share, and whether anyone feels threatened (particularly by the leader). The workbook is not to be used punitively! Honesty, warmth, and acceptance of each other are critical. We are all faulty. Even the apostle Paul in his later years wrote "Christ Jesus came into the world to save sinners – of whom I am the worst." (I Timothy 1:15-16). Paul did not say he "was" the worst of sinners; he said I "am" the worst. We are all faulty.

After the discussion, the father might ask each person how they felt about the lesson; some changes in format or pace may be needed. The family can then pray together in turn at the end of the lesson.

Some things to avoid are: children competing with each other, arguments or criticism of other's answers, and one person pointing out the faults of another. If someone does not recognize his own faults from the study, let God use His word in the Proverbs to convict that person of his or her weakness.

The wife should be careful to maintain a supportive role, because the whole purpose of the study will be defeated if arguments develop between the two parents. Single moms and mothers whose husbands are not able to participate can also use this workbook effectively.

One last caution: There seem to be two classic responses to Proverbs. One person sees the wisdom of Proverbs as too hard and too much to try; they walk away depressed and defeated before even trying God's wisdom. The other person sees the wisdom of Proverbs as a great challenge, requiring many corrections in his life, and walks away wanting to start trying.

Encourage the first person that God loves him or her just as they are, through their faith in Jesus Christ. This person often does not want to try wisdom because he expects failure and then rejection from God. The failure would be to not even try. This person must ask God from the heart, confessing the fear, to be strong in his life as he/she starts to trust God's wisdom over his/her own. The key to all obedience is dependence upon God. God will be faithful.

Our family used the workbook when our children were 8 and 10 years old. Younger children may need help to understand the questions and words. Definitions of some key words are included at the back of the workbook. The King James Version was originally used to prepare this workbook in 1980, but it has been rewritten for the New International Version. Other translations (New King James, New American Standard, New Living Translation etc.) may be helpful.

Older children and adults will find no problem in being challenged by the material. These issues are in the heart, not the mind. I have taught this material to adults in four different churches of four different denominations, in three different cities. In one case the principal of a local Christian high school who heard this teaching asked that I work with a high school teacher to make this teaching available to a senior class on practical living.

Richard S. Hockett
San Jose, California

Table of Contents

Lesson 1. What are Proverbs for?.. 13
Lesson 2. What does a wise person think about Proverbs? 15
Lesson 3. What does the unwise or foolish person think about Proverbs?...................... 16
Lesson 4. What attitude do we need to get help from Proverbs? 17
Lesson 5. Do we really need help from Proverbs? 19
Lesson 6. What are the blessings from obeying the wisdom of Proverbs? 21
Lesson 7. What can happen when we ignore the wisdom of Proverbs? 23
Lesson 8. The tongue: why not tell the truth? 24
Lesson 9. The tongue: righteous or wicked? 26
Lesson 10. The tongue: do you speak too much or too quickly? 28
Lesson 11. The tongue: do you have a wise tongue or a foolish tongue? 30
Lesson 12. The tongue: peaceful and not so peaceful? 32
Lesson 13. How do you handle the oppressor?... 34
Lesson 14. Why not get angry? 36
Lesson 15. I'm not a simple person! I just get into a lot of trouble because I believe everybody. 38
Lesson 16. I'm not a mocker! I just get angry whenever someone corrects me. 41
Lesson 17. I'm not a fool! I just don't particularly care about all this wisdom stuff. 44
Lesson 18. I don't want to tell someone about my sin. It's too embarrassing!................ 49
Lesson 19. How do you feel about being corrected? 52
Lesson 20. Do you ever think your way is right? 55
Lesson 21. Would you like a lot of money? What would you do with it?........................ 58
Lesson 22. Are you proud? Of what? 61
Lesson 23. The fear of the Lord. Why is it so important? 64
Lesson 24. Are you lazy?... 67
Lesson 25. Would you like to be diligent? 70
Lesson 26. How can parents help their children?.. 71
Lesson 27. Should I choose my friends? How? 76
Lesson 28. What is a leader? 78
Lesson 29. For men and boys: dangers of the adulteress... 81
Lesson 30. The Virtuous Woman... 86
Simple definitions of key words.. 89
Verses to memorize 91

Lesson 1. What are Proverbs for?

Read chapter 1 of Proverbs. Choose a verse that you especially like for sharing with your family. Begin to memorize 1:1-7 and James 3:13-17

(You will have four lessons' time to memorize these)

The reason the Proverbs were written by King Solomon is given in 1:1-4. This is what they are for.
**1 The proverbs of Solomon son of David, king of Israel:
2 for attaining wisdom and discipline; for understanding words of insight;
3 for acquiring a disciplined and prudent life, doing what is right and just and fair;
4 for giving prudence to the simple, knowledge and discretion to the young.**

Have you ever wondered whether something was right? There are some questions below. Put a check next to each question you have had before.

If you have had questions like these, then like the rest of us, you need help to know what is right. You need wisdom from God. You need the wisdom in Proverbs.

Some questions that wisdom can help you answer
____1. Should you say whatever you feel like saying?
____2. What should you do when someone picks on you?
____3. How are you supposed to feel when someone tells you did something wrong?
____4. Is there anything wrong with trying to make a lot of money?
____5. Can anybody, including you, be a leader?
____6. Can we be friends with anyone we like?
____7. Isn't being humble really being weak?
____8. Is talking a lot wrong?
____9. Why don't you always get wisdom when you want it?
___10. Should you be careful with your things or are some people just born to be careless?
___11. If you really feel something is right, should you go ahead and do it?
___12. Is it OK to get mad sometimes?
___13. How should you feel about money?
___14. What should you do with your money?
___15. What's wrong with sleeping a lot?
___16. Isn't it OK to be proud of some things?
___17. Do you have to want to obey God before you can get wisdom?
___18. Parents, are you raising your daughter right?
___19. What kind of woman does your son think about for a marriage partner?
___20. When should you say what's true, and when should you keep quiet?
___21. Should you believe everything people tell you?

___22. Is confession of your sin to people important?
___23. How can you tell if something should be said?

Proverbs will help you answer these questions, whether you are young or old.
They help you to know what is right
   to know what is just
   to know what is fair.

They help you to see ahead of time what to do, or what not to do.

Proverbs teaches us and sometimes corrects us too.
God's wisdom is often very different from man's wisdom.
Prov 14:12 There is a way that seems right to a man, but in the end it leads to death.

How do you think Proverbs could help you?

How does James 3:17 help you to know if something is wise to do or say?
James 3:17 But the wisdom that comes from heaven is first of all pure; then peace-loving, considerate, submissive, full of mercy and good fruit, impartial and sincere.

Lesson 2. What does a wise person think about Proverbs?

Read chapter 2 and choose a verse to share
Continue to memorize Proverbs 1:1-7 and James 3:13-17

A wise person really cares about Proverbs and the things it teaches him or her. Remember what Proverbs teach? See 1:1-4 in Lesson 1.

Read the following verses to learn more about what a wise person thinks about Proverbs and the things it teaches. In each verse, underline <u>one word or phrase</u> which tells how the wise person feels about the things Proverbs teaches.

For example, in 1:5 you would underline <u>listen</u>... the wise person is willing to hear what Proverbs has to say.

1:5 Let the wise listen and add to their learning, and let the discerning get guidance.

9: 8-9 Do not rebuke a mocker or he will hate you; rebuke a wise man and he will love you. Instruct a wise man and he will be wiser still; teach a righteous man and he will add to his learning.

10: 8 The wise in heart accept commands, but a chattering fool comes to ruin.

12:15 The way of a fool seems right to him, but a wise man listens to advice.

13:1 A wise son heeds his father's instruction, but a mocker does not listen to rebuke.

18:15 The heart of the discerning acquires knowledge; the ears of the wise seek it out.

What do you think about Proverbs?

Are you like the wise person?

Write an example of when you were like a wise person when someone corrected you or instructed you.

Lesson 3. What does an unwise or foolish person think about Proverbs?

Read chapter 3. Choose a verse to share.
Continue to memorize Proverbs 1:1-7 and James 3:13-17

An unwise or foolish person does not care about Proverbs and the things it teaches. (Remember what Proverbs teach? 1:1-4)

The following verses show what a **foolish** person thinks about Proverbs and the things it teaches. In each of these verses, underline a word or phrase which show how the foolish person feels about the things Proverbs teaches.

1:7 The fear of the LORD is the beginning of knowledge, but fools despise wisdom and discipline.

1:22 "How long will you simple ones love your simple ways? How long will mockers delight in mockery and fools hate knowledge?

15:5 A fool spurns his father's discipline, but whoever heeds correction shows prudence.

17:16 Of what use is money in the hand of a fool, since he has no desire to get wisdom?

18:2 A fool finds no pleasure in understanding but delights in airing his own opinions.

23:9 Do not speak to a fool, for he will scorn the wisdom of your words.

Do you see a difference between a wise person (Lesson 2) and a foolish person?
What is the difference?

Are you sometimes like the foolish person?

Write an example of when you were like a foolish person when someone corrected you or instructed you?

Lesson 4. What attitude do we need to get help from Proverbs?

Read chapter 4 and choose a verse to share.

James 1:5-8
If any of you lacks wisdom, he should ask God, who gives generously to all without finding fault, and it will be given to him. But when he asks, he must believe and not doubt, because he who doubts is like a wave of the sea, blown and tossed by the wind. That man should not think he will receive anything from the Lord; he is a double-minded man, unstable in all he does.

Be able to quote Proverbs 1:1-7 and James 3:13-17

Remember from Lesson 2 what the wise person thought about Proverbs and the things it teaches? Write out below the words underlined in Lesson 2.

These words describe the attitude we need to get help from Proverbs. (Your attitude is how you feel about something).

Proverbs 2:1-6 also describes this attitude. Read these verses very carefully and underline two words in each verse from 1-4 which shows how the person feels about God's wisdom.

1 My son, if you accept my words and store up my commands within you, 2 turning your ear to wisdom and applying your heart to understanding, 3 and if you call out for insight and cry aloud for understanding, 4 and if you look for it as for silver and search for it as for hidden treasure, 5 then you will understand the fear of the LORD and find the knowledge of God. 6 For the LORD gives wisdom, and from his mouth come knowledge and understanding.

What parts of the body or person are involved in 2:2-4?

How valuable should the wisdom of Proverbs be to us? (2:4)

How badly do you think we are to want the things Proverbs teaches (2:1-4)

Can you thing of anything more important to have?

Are any of these things more important than God's wisdom?

money?	awesome car?
friends?	pretty clothes?
beautiful house?	Ipad?
good grades?	a pet?
rewards?	books?
good looks?	toys?
beauty?	bicycle?
health?	sports?
a fun job?	swimming?
power?	anything else?

If we have the attitude of Proverbs 2:1-4, what will we get?

5 then you will understand the fear of the LORD and find the knowledge of God. 6 For the LORD gives wisdom, and from his mouth come knowledge and understanding.

What can you do to show God that you want the wisdom that Proverbs teaches?

Lesson 5. Do we really need help from Proverbs?

>Read chapter 5 and choose a verse to share.
>Memorize Proverbs 3:13.

We really do need help from Proverbs. Sometimes we don't get along with others. Maybe we said something wrong to them, but did not mean to. Or maybe we did something nasty to them and then wished we could take it back.

Sometimes we may want to help someone else who has a problem acting badly. But we don't know what to do to help.

Sometimes someone picks on us and we don't know what to do.
Sometimes we are unhappy because we don't have enough money.
Sometimes we are unhappy because someone hurt our pride or we are embarrassed.
Sometimes we get mad when someone corrects us.
Sometimes, many times we need help.
We always need help to please the Lord.

The following verses show some ways that Proverbs can help us. Study them carefully.

1:33 But whoever listens to me will live in safety and be at ease, without fear of harm.

2:10-12 For wisdom will enter your heart, and knowledge will be pleasant to your soul.
Discretion will protect you, and understanding will guard you.
Wisdom will save you from the ways of wicked men, from men whose words are perverse

2:16 It will save you also from the adulteress, from the wayward wife with her seductive words

2:20 Thus you will walk in the ways of good men and keep to the paths of the righteous.

3:4 Then you will win favor and a good name in the sight of God and man.

2:5 Then you will understand the fear of the LORD and find the knowledge of God.

3:5-6 Trust in the LORD with all your heart and lean not on your own understanding; in all your ways acknowledge him, and he will direct your paths.

3:13 Blessed is the man who finds wisdom, the man who gains understanding.

Colossians 1:9-10
>For this reason ... we have not stopped praying for you and asking God to fill you
>>with the knowledge of his will
>>>through all spiritual wisdom and understanding.
>>And we pray this in order that you may live a life worthy of the Lord
>>>and may please him in every way:
>>bearing fruit in every good work
>>growing in the knowledge of God

Which of these verses show that wisdom protects us? (give the references)

Which verses show that wisdom helps us to please God?

Which verses show that wisdom guides us?

Which verses show that wisdom helps us to be happy?

Which verses show that wisdom helps us to know God better?

Put an X next to those things below where you need help from Proverbs...

____ attitude to correction
____ pride
____ money
____ protection from mean people
____ how to help people
____ not saying the wrong thing
____ saying the right thing
____ choosing friends
____ making friends
____ how to please God
____ not sleeping too much
____ being happy
____ staying out of trouble
____ being a leader
____ something else? (write it out here)

Lesson 6. What are the blessings from obeying the wisdom of Proverbs?

>Read chapter 6. Share a verse
>Memorize Proverbs 3:3-4

There are many blessings from obeying the wisdom of Proverbs. In the first 4 chapters you can find many of these blessings that come from following wisdom. Underline the blessings described in the following verses:

1:33 but whoever listens to me [wisdom] will live in safety and be at ease, without fear of harm.

2:10-12 For wisdom will enter your heart, and knowledge will be pleasant to your soul. Discretion will protect you, and understanding will guard you. Wisdom will save you from the ways of wicked men, from men whose words are perverse,

2:16 It [wisdom] will save you also from the adulteress, from the wayward wife with her seductive words,

2:20 Thus you will walk in the ways of good men and keep to the paths of the righteous.

3:2 ...for they [my commands] will prolong your life many years and bring you prosperity

3:4 Then you will win favor and a good name in the sight of God and man.

3:8 This will bring health to your body and nourishment to your bones.

3:16 Long life is in her [wisdom's} right hand; in her left hand are riches and honor.

3:17 Her [wisdom's] ways are pleasant ways, and all her paths are peace,

3:18 She [wisdom] is a tree of life to those who embrace her; those who lay hold of her will be blessed.

3:22 They will be life for you, an ornament to grace your neck.

3:23 Then you will go on your way in safety, and your foot will not stumble.

3:24 When you lie down, you will not be afraid; when you lie down, your sleep will be sweet.

3:26 ... for the LORD will be your confidence and will keep your foot from being snared.

4:8 Esteem her [wisdom], and she will exalt you; embrace her, and she will honor you.

4:9 She [wisdom] will set a garland of grace on your head and present you with a crown of splendor.

4:12   When you walk, your steps will not be hampered; when you run, you will not stumble.

Another blessing from Proverbs is found in 19:23:
The fear of the LORD leads to life: Then one rests content, untouched by trouble.

Which four of the blessings of Proverbs do you want most? Why?
1.

2.

3.

4.

Do you want to obey the wisdom of Proverbs?

Lesson 7. What can happen when we ignore the wisdom of Proverbs?

    Read chapter 7. Choose a verse to share.
    Memorize 1:28-29.

Trouble and problems can come when we ignore the wisdom of Proverbs.

Read carefully 1:24-32.
24 But since you rejected me [wisdom] when I called and no one gave heed when I stretched out my hand, 25 since you ignored all my advice and would not accept my rebuke, 26 I in turn will laugh at your disaster; I will mock when calamity overtakes you—27 when calamity overtakes you like a storm, when disaster sweeps over you like a whirlwind, when distress and trouble overwhelm you. 28 "Then they will call to me but I will not answer; they will look for me but will not find me. 29 Since they hated knowledge and did not choose to fear the LORD, 30 since they would not accept my advice and spurned my rebuke, 31 they will eat the fruit of their ways and be filled with the fruit of their schemes. 32 For the waywardness of the simple will kill them, and the complacency of fools will destroy them.

Can you summarize this in your own words?

These verses warn us. If we decide to ignore wisdom, trouble can come. Then if we decide to call out for wisdom when in trouble, wisdom may not come to help us. This is serious.

Psalm 107 teaches us that when we get into trouble and finally decide to give up and let God deliver us, then He will. But we should never ignore wisdom and just think God will get us out of our trouble.

Read Psalms 107:17-22 :
17 Some became fools through their rebellious ways and suffered affliction because of their iniquities. 18 They loathed all food and drew near the gates of death. 19 Then they cried to the LORD in their trouble, and he saved them from their distress. 20 He sent forth his word and healed them; he rescued them from the grave. 21 Let them give thanks to the LORD for his unfailing love and his wonderful deeds for men. 22 Let them sacrifice thank offerings and tell of his works with songs of joy.

Give an example of when you got into trouble for not being wise.

Do you want to obey or ignore the wisdom of Proverbs?

Lesson 8. The tongue: why not tell the truth?

    Read chapter 8. Choose a verse to share.
    Memorize 12:19.

What we say shows a great deal about us! Sometimes what we say tells people about us—just what we don't want them to know!

That sounds very strange, doesn't it?

But the Lord Jesus said,
    "For out of the overflow of the heart the mouth speaks." (Matthew 12:34)

You see, what my mouth speaks really tells people what my heart is like. If I speak unkindly, it is because my heart is unkind. If I lie, or flatter, or talk as a hypocrite, then people will know that I have the heart of a liar, or a flatterer, or a hypocrite.

That's scary, isn't it?

Let's see what God's wisdom says about telling the truth, lying, flattery, and hypocrisy.

<u>Telling the truth</u> (underline the result of telling the truth)
12:17 A truthful witness gives honest testimony, but a false witness tells lies.

12:19 Truthful lips endure forever, but a lying tongue lasts only a moment.

12:22 The LORD detests lying lips, but he delights in men who are truthful.

16:13 Kings take pleasure in honest lips; they value a man who speaks the truth.

23:16 My inmost being will rejoice when your lips speak what is right.

<u>A lying tongue</u> (underline the result of lying)
6:16-19 There are six things the LORD hates, seven that are detestable to him: haughty eyes, a lying tongue, hands that shed innocent blood, a heart that devises wicked schemes, feet that are quick to rush into evil, a false witness who pours out lies and a man who stirs up dissension among brothers.

Lesson 8. The tongue: why not tell the truth?

10:18 He who conceals his hatred has lying lips, and whoever spreads slander is a fool.

12:19 Truthful lips endure forever, but a lying tongue lasts only a moment.

17:7 Arrogant lips are unsuited to a fool— how much worse lying lips to a ruler!

19:5 A false witness will not go unpunished, and he who pours out lies will not go free.

26:28 A lying tongue hates those it hurts, and a flattering mouth works ruin.

Flattery (underline the result of flattery)
26:28 A lying tongue hates those it hurts, and a flattering mouth works ruin.

29:5 Whoever flatters his neighbor is spreading a net for his feet.

28:23 He who rebukes a man will in the end gain more favor than he who has a flattering tongue.

Godless (KJV – hypocrite) (underline the result)
11:9 With his mouth the godless destroys his neighbor, but through knowledge the righteous escape.

Why do we sometimes tell a lie rather than the truth?

Have you ever told a lie? What for?

Why is it hard sometimes to tell the truth?

Lesson 9. The tongue: righteous or wicked?

    Read chapter 9 and choose a verse to share.
    Memorize Proverbs 10:11.

Proverbs talks about the tongue of the righteous or just person. It also talks about the tongue of people called wicked and perverse (that means evil, mean or nasty).

Righteous tongue/mouth (underline the result of the righteous tongue)
10:11 The mouth of the righteous is a fountain of life, but violence overwhelms the mouth of the wicked.

10:20-21 The tongue of the righteous is choice silver, but the heart of the wicked is of little value. The lips of the righteous nourish many, but fools die for lack of judgment

10:31 The mouth of the righteous brings forth wisdom, but a perverse tongue will be cut out.

10:32 The lips of the righteous know what is fitting, but the mouth of the wicked only what is perverse.

Wicked tongue/mouth (underline the results of wicked or evil tongue)
10:11 The mouth of the righteous is a fountain of life, but violence overwhelms the mouth of the wicked.

12:6 The words of the wicked lie in wait for blood, but the speech of the upright rescues them.

12:13 An evil man is trapped by his sinful talk, but a righteous man escapes trouble.

24:1-2 Do not envy wicked men, do not desire their company; for their hearts plot violence, and their lips talk about making trouble,

Perverse tongue (underline the results of this tongue; perverse = evil, mean, nasty)
4:24 Put away perversity from your mouth; keep corrupt talk far from your lips.

8:13 To fear the LORD is to hate evil; I hate pride and arrogance, evil behavior and perverse speech.

15:4 The tongue that brings healing is a tree of life, but a deceitful tongue crushes the spirit.

17:20 A man of perverse heart does not prosper; he whose tongue is deceitful falls into trouble.

Lesson 9. The tongue: righteous or wicked?

19:1 Better a poor man whose walk is blameless than a fool whose lips are perverse.

What does your tongue sound like?

Give examples of when your tongue sounded like:

       the righteous tongue   the "other" tongue

Lesson 10. The tongue: do you speak too much or too quickly?

Read chapter 10 (there is much here on the tongue). Choose a verse to share.
Memorize 10:19.

Sometimes we talk too much. Sometimes we speak too quickly when something happens and then wish we had waited.

Proverbs teaches us that "holding our tongue" is wise. That means being careful what we say and sometimes deciding not to say anything at all.

Holding your tongue   (underline good results)
10:19 When words are many, sin is not absent, but he who holds his tongue is wise.

11:12-13 A man who lacks judgment derides his neighbor, but a man of understanding holds his tongue. A gossip betrays a confidence, but a trustworthy man keeps a secret.

13:3 He who guards his lips guards his life, but he who speaks rashly will come to ruin.

17:27-28 A man of knowledge uses words with restraint, and a man of understanding is even-tempered. Even a fool is thought wise if he keeps silent, and discerning if he holds his tongue.

Talking too much   (underline bad results)
10:19 When words are many, sin is not absent, but he who holds his tongue is wise.

13:3 He who guards his lips guards his life, but he who speaks rashly will come to ruin.

14:23 All hard work brings a profit, but mere talk leads only to poverty.

Speaking in haste   (underline bad results)
29:20 Do you see a man who speaks in haste? There is more hope for a fool than for him.

Why is it hard sometimes to keep quiet, rather than going ahead and talking?

Lesson 10. The tongue: do you speak too much or too quickly?

Do you sometimes talk too much without really saying anything important? Give an example.

Do you sometimes speak in haste (too quickly) when something happens? Do you speak before you think? Do you interrupt people?
Give an example of speaking in haste.

Now give an example of when you held back saying something or decided to listen rather than talk.

Lesson 11. The tongue: do you have a wise tongue or a foolish tongue?

   Read chapter 11. Choose a verse to share.
   Memorize 12:18.

Proverbs has much to say about the tongue of the wise and the tongue of the fool.

Wise tongue   (underline good results)
12:18 Reckless words pierce like a sword, but the tongue of the wise brings healing.

14:3 A fool's talk brings a rod to his back, but the lips of the wise protect them.

15:2 The tongue of the wise commends knowledge, but the mouth of the fool gushes folly.

15:7 The lips of the wise spread knowledge; not so the hearts of fools.

16:23 A wise man's heart guides his mouth, and his lips promote instruction.

Foolish tongue   (underline bad results)
10:14 Wise men store up knowledge, but the mouth of a fool invites ruin.

12:23 A prudent man keeps his knowledge to himself, but the heart of fools blurts out folly.

14:3 A fool's talk brings a rod to his back, but the lips of the wise protect them.

14:7 Stay away from a foolish man, for you will not find knowledge on his lips.

15:2 The tongue of the wise commends knowledge, but the mouth of the fool gushes folly.

15:7 The lips of the wise spread knowledge; not so the hearts of fools.

18:6-7 A fool's lips bring him strife, and his mouth invites a beating. A fool's mouth is his undoing, and his lips are a snare to his soul.

Why would we want to speak like a fool rather than like a wise person?

Lesson 11. The tongue: do you have a wise tongue or a foolish tongue?

Would a wise person talk back or say smart remarks to get back?

Would a wise person make fun of someone he did not like?

Give an example of when your tongue sounded:

<u>wise</u>   <u>foolish</u>

Which kind of tongue do <u>you</u> want?

Lesson 12. The tongue: peaceful and not so peaceful

Read chapter 12 (there is much here on the tongue). Choose a verse to share.
Memorize 15:1.

Proverbs says much about peaceful and non-peaceful uses of the tongue.

Peaceful Tongue   (underline results)
12:25 An anxious heart weighs a man down, but a kind word cheers him up.

15:1 A gentle answer turns away wrath, but a harsh word stirs up anger.

15:4 The tongue that brings healing is a tree of life, but a deceitful tongue crushes the spirit.

15:23 A man finds joy in giving an apt reply— and how good is a timely word!
(New Living Transation: Everyone enjoys a fitting reply; it is wonderful to say the right thing at the right time!)

16:24 Pleasant words are a honeycomb, sweet to the soul and healing to the bones.

22:11 He who loves a pure heart and whose speech is gracious will have the king for his friend.

25:11 A word aptly [or "fitly" KJV, ESV] spoken is like apples of gold in settings of silver.

Non-peaceful tongue   (underline bad results)
15:1 A gentle answer turns away wrath, but a harsh word stirs up anger.

11:13 A gossip betrays a confidence, but a trustworthy man keeps a secret.

16.28 A perverse man stirs up dissension, and a gossip separates close friends.

18:8 The words of a gossip are like choice morsels; they go down to a man's inmost parts.

26:20 Without wood a fire goes out; without gossip a quarrel dies down.

20:20 A gossip betrays a confidence; so avoid a man who talks too much.

26:24-25 A malicious man disguises himself with his lips, but in his heart he harbors deceit. Though his speech is charming, do not believe him, for seven abominations fill his heart.

27:2 Let another praise you, and not your own mouth; someone else, and not your own lips.

Lesson 12. The tongue: peaceful and not so peaceful

___

What do you think Proverbs 18:21 means? *(see below)*
"The tongue has the power of life and death, and those who love it will eat its fruit."

Does your tongue sound peaceful or non-peaceful? Give examples of your tongue speaking in both ways.

Would a peaceful tongue show quick anger at somebody?

Do you believe you should think before speaking and decide to say only things that are peaceful?

Remember what James 3:17 says about God's wisdom…
But the wisdom that comes from heaven is first of all pure; then peace-loving, considerate, submissive, full of mercy and good fruit, impartial and sincere.

Is it always peaceable (peace-loving)?

Lesson 13. How do you handle the oppressor?

An oppressor is a person who picks on you or pushes you around...a bully.

Read chapter 13 and choose a verse to share.

Memorize Proverbs 3:31-32: **Do not envy a violent man or choose any of his ways, for the LORD detests a perverse man but takes the upright into his confidence.**
(Father: see in Psalm 18 how David recognized God's hand in delivering him)

How do you handle the oppressor? You don't. You let God handle the oppressor.

Do you sometimes want to be like the oppressor?

What does 3:31-32 say about wanting to be like the oppressor?

Why should you not be like the oppressor?

Do you sometimes want to get back at someone who is picking on you?

What do the following proverbs say about that?

20:22 Do not say, "I'll pay you back for this wrong!" Wait for the LORD, and he will deliver you.

24:29 Do not say, "I'll do to him as he has done to me; I'll pay that man back for what he did."

Should you count on your own strength (your quick tongue or fast fists) to protect you from the oppressor? Look at the following proverbs:
21:31 The horse is made ready for the day of battle, but victory rests with the LORD.

3:25-26 Have no fear of sudden disaster or of the ruin that overtakes the wicked, for the LORD will be your confidence and will keep your foot from being snared.

How should you act when someone picks on you?
25:21-22 If your enemy is hungry, give him food to eat; if he is thirsty, give him water to drink. In doing this, you will heap burning coals on his head, and the LORD will reward you.

Should you be happy when the oppressor gets into trouble?
24:17-18 Do not gloat when your enemy falls; when he stumbles, do not let your heart rejoice, or the LORD will see and disapprove and turn his wrath away from him.

Be sure you aren't the one who starts a fight.
17:14 Starting a quarrel is like breaching a dam; so drop the matter before a dispute breaks out.

28:25 A greedy man stirs up dissension, but he who trusts in the LORD will prosper.

I think we want to be like the oppressor for two reasons.
First he seems to get his way and we don't.

Second, if he picks on us and we don't fight back, it makes us look weak; it hurts our pride. Do you agree?

Does he really get his way?
(Father: see Psalms 73)

Are we really weak if we don't fight back?
(Father: see example of Christ in 1 Pet 2:21-23)

Lesson 14. Why not get angry?

    Read chapter 14.   Share a verse
    Memorize Proverbs 15:18.

Why not get angry? There are several reasons

First, to be slow to anger shows great strength and great understanding. What do the following verses say about being slow to anger or wrath?
14:29 A patient man has great understanding, but a quick-tempered man displays folly.

16:32 Better a patient man than a warrior, a man who controls his temper than one who takes a city.

Who is stronger than a warrior?
Second, to overlook an offense shows wisdom, brings glory, and calms a quarrel. What do these proverbs say?
15:18 A hot-tempered man stirs up dissension, but a patient man calms a quarrel.

19:11 A man's wisdom gives him patience; it is to his glory to overlook an offense.

Third, to act in anger will only cause dissension or argument. It never helps to correct the situation. What do the following proverbs tell us?
29:22 An angry man stirs up dissension, and a hot-tempered one commits many sins.

10:12 Hatred stirs up dissension, but love covers over all wrongs.

15:18 A hot-tempered man stirs up dissension, but a patient man calms a quarrel.

15:1 A gentle answer turns away wrath, but a harsh word stirs up anger.

Fourth, to get angry quickly shows that you are a fool. What does this say?
14:17 A quick-tempered man does foolish things, and a crafty man is hated.

Why do you get angry when you do? Check one or more of the following: (You may substitute He and She)

   ____ He said something untrue about me.
   ____ He took something of mine.
   ____ She would not let me have my way.
   ____ He punched me.
   ____ They made fun of me.
   ____ He did not get caught for doing wrong.

Lesson 14. Why not get angry?

___ She thought I was stupid.
___ He would not listen to me.
___ She had no business correcting me.
___ They should be punished.
___ She wouldn't understand what I was saying.
___ He insulted me.
___ Things don't work.
___Things get lost.
___ He was careless and broke it.
___ The kids just won't do what they're told.
___ This project is just so frustrating (work project, home project, homework, etc.)
___ He cheated and won't admit it.
___ Something else?

We might look into the Bible and discover why the reasons above are not good reasons for getting angry, but that would take us far away from our Proverbs study. The proverbs that we have looked at just teach us that anger in general is not wise.

If we think God is wiser than we are, we should follow his wisdom about anger, rather than our feelings.

Lesson 15. I'm not a simple person! I just get into a lot of trouble because I believe everybody

Read chapter 15. Choose a verse to share.
Memorize 22:3.

Proverbs calls to three kinds of people who do not really want God's wisdom. In the first chapter wisdom cries out:

> "How long will you simple ones love your simple ways?
> How long will mockers delight in mockery
> And fools hate knowledge?
> If you had responded to my rebuke,
> I would have poured out my heart to you
> and made my thoughts known to you." (1:22-23)

The three kinds of people are called simple ones, mockers, and fools. Proverbs talks a lot about these three kinds of people. You may be like one of them or like all of them at one time or another.

Learning what Proverbs says about these three kinds of people will help you understand yourself and others. It will really help you to change the way you act when someone corrects you with God's wisdom.

This lesson will be on the simple person. Below is a list of all the Proverbs about the simple person. Let's see if we can understand this person.

PROVERBS ON THE SIMPLE

1:22 How long will you simple ones love your simple ways? ...
1:1, 4 The proverbs of Solomon.... to give prudence to the simple
7:7   I saw among the simple, I noticed among the young men, a youth who lacked judgment. (in regards to going to a prostitute)
8:5   You who are simple, gain prudence; you who are foolish, gain understanding.
9:1-6 Wisdom has built her house; she has hewn out its seven pillars. She has prepared her meat and mixed her wine; she has also set her table. She has sent out her maids, and she calls from the highest point of the city. "Let all who are simple come in here!" she says to those who lack judgment. "Come, eat my food and drink the wine I have mixed. Leave your simple ways and you will live; walk in the way of understanding.
9:13-18 The woman Folly is loud; she is undisciplined and without knowledge. She sits at the door of her house, on a seat at the highest point of the city, calling out to those who pass by, who go straight on their way. "Let all who are simple come in here!" she says to those who

Lesson 15. I'm not a simple person! I just get into a lot of trouble because I believe everybody

lack judgment. "Stolen water is sweet; food eaten in secret is delicious!" But little do they know that the dead are there, that her guests are in the depths of the grave.
14:15   A simple man believes anything, but a prudent man gives thought to his steps.
14:18   The simple inherit folly: but the prudent are crowned with knowledge.
19:25   Flog a mocker, and the simple will learn prudence...
21:11   When a mocker is punished, the simple gain wisdom...
22:3   A prudent man sees danger and takes refuge, but the simple keep going and suffer for it.

Answer the following questions and put a reference in parenthesis to show which verse or verses you used to get the answer. The first question is answered for you as an example.

1. What kind of person is the opposite of a simple person?
   Answer: a prudent person (14:15, 18; 22:3)

2. Does a simple person believe everything people tell him?

3. Does a simple person foresee evil (does he see ahead of time that trouble will happen if he chooses to do something?)

4. Why does a simple person get into trouble?

5. What does a simple person think of his being simple?

6. What do 19:25 and 21:11 say about the simple and the mocker? What do you think that is all about?

7. How can a simple person get help? Read Psalms 107:4-9.
   (A simple person wanders around not knowing where to find wisdom.)
   Some wandered in desert wastelands, finding no way to a city where they could settle. They were hungry and thirsty, and their lives ebbed away. Then they cried out to the LORD in their trouble, and he delivered them from their distress. He led them by a straight way to a city where they could settle. Let them give thanks to the LORD for his unfailing love and his wonderful deeds for men, for He satisfies the thirsty and fills the hungry with good things.

Are you like a simple person in some ways?
List the ways you are alike.

Give an example of when you were like the simple person.

How can you get help?

Are you going to get help? Or are you just going to think about getting help?

Father: See how Abram was a simple person following the advice of his wife who was a mocker. Genesis 16:1-6

Lesson 16. I'm not a mocker! I just get very angry whenever someone corrects me.

    Read chapter 16. Choose a verse to share.
    Memorize 3:34.

This lesson is on the second person wisdom calls to (1:22-23).

Below are listed all the Proverbs about the <u>mocker</u>. Let's see if we can understand this person.

PROVERBS ON THE MOCKER

1:22 How long will mockers delight in mockery…?

3:34 He mocks proud mockers but gives grace to the humble.

9:7, 8 Whoever corrects a mocker invites insult; whoever rebukes a wicked man incurs abuse. Do not rebuke a mocker or he will hate you; rebuke a wise man and he will love you.

9:12 If you are wise, your wisdom will reward you; if you are a mocker, you alone will suffer.

13:1 A wise son heeds his father's instruction, but a mocker does not listen to rebuke.

14:6 The mocker seeks wisdom and finds none, but knowledge comes easily to the discerning.

15:12 A mocker resents correction; he will not consult the wise.

19:25 Flog a mocker, and the simple will learn prudence…

19:28 A corrupt witness mocks at justice, and the mouth of the wicked gulps down evil.

21:11 When a mocker is punished, the simple gain wisdom…

22:10 Drive out the mocker, and out goes strife; quarrels and insults are ended.

24:9 The schemes of folly are sin, and men detest a mocker.

29:8 Mockers stir up a city, but wise men turn away anger.

Answer the following questions and give the verse or verses where you found your answer.

1. What does a mocker think of being corrected (or rebuked) and the person correcting him?

2. What does a mocker think about his mocking?
   Does he think it is wrong?

3. Does a mocker want to be wise?

4. Why do you think a person like the mocker (who wants to be wise) can't find wisdom? (This is an opinion question)

5. Will a mocker go to a truly wise person for wisdom?

6. What does God think of the mocker?

7. Do you think a mocker gets into a lot of arguments?

8. Do you think a mocker has any good friends?

9. What happens when a mocker is punished?

10. What should be done with a mocker?

11. How can a mocker get help?

Are you like the mocker in some ways? List the ways you are alike.

Give an example of when you were like a mocker.

Lesson 16. I'm not a mocker! I just get very angry whenever someone corrects me.

Do you have trouble finding wisdom or do you already think you are wise?

Do you have trouble keeping friends after people get to know you?

If you are a mocker, what is God doing now?

What should you do? Read Psalms 107:10-16.
(One who rebels against the counsel of the Most High is a mocker.)

Some sat in darkness and the deepest gloom, prisoners suffering in iron chains, for they had rebelled against the words of God and despised the counsel of the Most High. So he subjected them to bitter labor; they stumbled, and there was no one to help. Then they cried to the LORD in their trouble, and he saved them from their distress. He brought them out of darkness and the deepest gloom and broke away their chains. Let them give thanks to the LORD for his unfailing love and his wonderful deeds for men, for He breaks down gates of bronze and cuts through bars of iron

Father: See how Jonah was a mocker before God in Jonah 1:1-3, 4:1-3.

Moses also mocked God when he struck the rock (Num 20:10,11) rather than speak to the rock as God had said (Num 20:8).

Lesson 17. I'm not a fool! I just don't particularly care about all this wisdom stuff.

    Read chapter 17 and choose a verse to share.
    Memorize 1:7.

This lesson is on the third person wisdom calls to (1:22-23). The next several pages list all the Proverbs about the fool and folly. Proverbs has a lot to say about the fool. *This is a long lesson and should be discussed over several periods of getting together.*

Answer the following questions and give the verse or verses where you found your answer.

1. What does a fool think of wisdom and instruction and knowledge?

2. What does a fool think about being a fool? (Would a fool *think* he was a fool?)

3. Is a fool proud?

4. Does a fool get into arguments?

5. Is it good to be friends with a fool?

6. Which verses show that the fool's problem has to do with his heart? (circle the word "heart" wherever you find it in the verses)

What do you think that means?

Lesson 17. I'm not a fool! I just don't particularly care about all this wisdom stuff.

PROVERBS ON THE FOOL

1:7 The fear of the LORD is the beginning of knowledge, but fools despise wisdom and discipline.
1:22 "How long will you simple ones love your simple ways? ...and fools hate knowledge?
1:32 For the waywardness of the simple will kill them, and the complacency of fools will destroy them;
3:35 The wise inherit honor, but fools he holds up to shame.
8:5 ...you who are foolish, gain understanding
9:13-18 The woman Folly is loud; she is undisciplined and without knowledge. She sits at the door of her house, on a seat at the highest point of the city, calling out to those who pass by, who go straight on their way. "Let all who are simple come in here!" she says to those who lack judgment. "Stolen water is sweet; food eaten in secret is delicious!" But little do they know that the dead are there, that her guests are in the depths of the grave.
10:1 A wise son makes a father glad, but a foolish son is a grief to his mother.
10:8 The wise of heart will receive commands, but a chattering fool comes to ruin.
10:10 He who winks maliciously causes grief, and a chattering fool comes to ruin.
10:14 Wise men store up knowledge, but the mouth of a fool invites ruin.
10:18 He who conceals hatred has lying lips, and he who spreads slander is a fool.
10:21 The lips of the righteous nourish many, but fools die for lack of judgment.
10:23 A fool finds pleasure in evil conduct, but a man of understanding delights in wisdom.
11:29 He who brings trouble on his on his own family will inherit only wind, and the foolish will be servant to the wise.
12:15 The way of a fool seems right to him, but a wise man listens to advice.
12:16 A fool shows his annoyance at once, but a prudent man overlooks an insult.
12:23 A prudent man keeps his knowledge to himself, but the heart of fools blurts out folly.
13:16 Every prudent man acts out of knowledge, but a fool exposes his folly.
13:19 A longing fulfilled is sweet to the soul, but fools detest turning from evil.
13:20 He who walks with the wise grows wise, but a companion of fools will suffer harm.
14:1 The wise woman builds her house, but with her own hands the foolish one tears hers down.
14:3 A fool's talk brings a rod to his back, but the lips of the wise protect them.
14:7 Stay away from a foolish man, for you will not find knowledge on his lips.
14:8 The wisdom of the prudent is to give thought to their ways, but the folly of fools is deception.
14:9 Fools mock at making amends for sin, but goodwill is found among the upright.
14:16 A wise man fears the LORD and shuns evil, but a fool is hotheaded and reckless.
14:17 A quick-tempered man does foolish things, and a crafty man is hated.
14:24 The wealth of the wise is their crown, but the folly of fools yields folly.
14:33 Wisdom reposes in the heart of the discerning and even among fools she lets herself be known.
15:2 The tongue of the wise commends knowledge, but the mouth of the fool gushes folly.
15:5 A fool spurns his father's discipline, but whoever heeds correction shows prudence.
15:7 The lips of the wise spread knowledge; not so the hearts of fools.
15:14 The discerning heart seeks knowledge, but the mouth of a fool feeds on folly.
15:20 A wise son brings joy to his father, but a foolish man despises his mother.
16:22 Understanding is a fountain of life to those who have it, but folly brings punishment to fools.
17:7 Arrogant lips are unsuited to a fool— how much worse lying lips to a ruler!
17:10 A rebuke impresses a man of discernment more than a hundred lashes a fool.
17:12 Better to meet a bear robbed of her cubs than a fool in his folly.
17:16 Of what use is money in the hand of a fool, since he has no desire to get wisdom?

17:21 To have a fool for a son brings grief; there is no joy for the father of a fool.
17:24 A discerning man keeps wisdom in view, but a fool's eyes wander to the ends of the earth.
17:25 A foolish son brings grief to his father and bitterness to the one who bore him.
17:28 Even a fool is thought wise if he keeps silent, and discerning if he holds his tongue.
18:2 A fool finds no pleasure in understanding but delights in airing his own opinions.
18:6 A fool's lips bring him strife, and his mouth invites a beating.
18:7 A fool's mouth is his undoing, and his lips are a snare to his soul.
19:1 Better a poor man whose walk is blameless than a fool whose lips are perverse.
19:3 A man's own folly ruins his life, yet his heart rages against the LORD.
19:10 It is not fitting for a fool to live in luxury— how much worse for a slave to rule over princes!
19:13 A foolish son is his father's ruin, and a quarrelsome wife is like a constant dripping.
19:29 Penalties are prepared for mockers, and beatings for the backs of fools.
20:3 It is to a man's honor to avoid strife, but every fool is quick to quarrel.
21:20 In the house of the wise are stores of choice food and oil, but a foolish man devours all he has.
22:15 Folly is bound up in the heart of a child, but the rod of discipline will drive it far from him.
23:9 Do not speak to a fool, for he will scorn the wisdom of your words.
24:7 Wisdom is too high for a fool; in the assembly at the gate he has nothing to say.
24:9 The schemes of folly are sin, and men detest a mocker.
26:1 Like snow in summer or rain in harvest, honor is not fitting for a fool.
26:3 A whip for the horse, a halter for the donkey, and a rod for the backs of fools!
26:4 Do not answer a fool according to his folly, or you will be like him yourself.
26:5 Answer a fool according to his folly, or he will be wise in his own eyes.
26:6 Like cutting off one's feet or drinking violence is the sending of a message by the hand of a fool.
26:7 Like a lame man's legs that hang limp is a proverb in the mouth of a fool.
26:8 Like tying a stone in a sling is the giving of honor to a fool.
26:9 Like a thorn bush in a drunkard's hand is a proverb in the mouth of a fool.
26:10 Like an archer who wounds at random is he who hires a fool or any passer-by.
26:11 As a dog returns to its vomit, so a fool repeats his folly.
26:12 Do you see a man wise in his own eyes? There is more hope for a fool than for him.
27:3 Stone is heavy and sand a burden, but provocation by a fool is heavier than both.
27:22 Though you grind a fool in a mortar, grinding him like grain with a pestle, you will not remove his folly from him.
28:26 He who trusts in himself is a fool, but he who walks in wisdom is kept safe.
29:9 If a wise man goes to court with a fool, the fool rages and scoffs, and there is no peace.
29:11 A fool gives full vent to his anger, but a wise man keeps himself under control.
29:20 Do you see a man who speaks in haste? There is more hope for a fool than for him.
30:21-22 Under three things the earth trembles, under four it cannot bear up: ...a fool who is full of food...
30:32 If you have played the fool and exalted yourself, or if you have planned evil, clap your hand over your mouth!

7 The fool seems to think that God (and His wisdom) has nothing to do with some parts of his life. Note the descriptions of the fool in the following Psalms:

Psalm 14:1 The fool says in his heart, "There is no God." They are corrupt, their deeds are vile; there is no one who does good.

Lesson 17. I'm not a fool! I just don't particularly care about all this wisdom stuff.

Psalm 94:7-9 They say, "The LORD does not see; the God of Jacob pays no heed." Take heed, you senseless ones among the people; you fools, when will you become wise? Does He who implanted the ear not hear? Does He who formed the eye not see?

8. As Christians we may not tell God He is to have nothing to do with our lives, but we may act as if certain parts of our lives are none of His business. Ephesians 5:15-17 shows that Christians can be fools or like fools.

> **Be very careful, then, how you live—not as unwise but as wise, making the most of every opportunity, because the days are evil. Therefore do not be foolish, but understand what the Lord's will is.**

9. Proverbs calls to the fool's heart (8:5) not his understanding. Maybe his heart needs to see again that he is under the authority of God. Some of the fool's actions show that he does not think God is watching and judging him.

10 Why does a fool get into trouble?

11 Does a fool want to depart from evil?

12 What should be done with a fool?

13. What can a fool do to get help? (Read Psalms 107:17-22)
Some became fools through their rebellious ways and suffered affliction because of their iniquities. They loathed all food and drew near the gates of death. Then they cried to the LORD in their trouble, and He saved them from their distress. He sent forth his word and healed them; He rescued them from the grave. Let them give thanks to the LORD for his unfailing love and His wonderful deeds for men. Let them sacrifice thank offerings and tell of His works with songs of joy.

Are you like a fool in some ways?
List the ways you are alike.

Give an example of when you were like a fool.

Do you want help? What are you going to do?

Father: See how David acted like a fool when he committed adultery and murder II Samuel 11-12. He acted like God was not watching him and judging him. God had to send His prophet Nathan to David to show him God knew and cared about David's wickedness.

Lesson 18. I don't want to tell someone about my sin. It's too embarrassing!

Read chapter 18 and choose a verse to share.
Memorize 28:13.

Confessing our sin to God and to people is very hard (admitting we did wrong).
It's embarrassing.
Or we think we'll get into trouble.
And then there is our pride!
Besides, every one else sins too; so why should we confess?

Proverbs does not agree with those excuses. Proverbs 28:13 says:

> "He who conceals his sins does not prosper,
> but whoever confesses and renounces them finds mercy."

What does I John 1:8-9 say?
If we claim to be without sin, we deceive ourselves and the truth is not in us. If we confess our sins, he is faithful and just and will forgive us our sins and purify us from all unrighteousness.

So if we cover our sin or refuse to admit we have it, God's word says we will not do well (28:13) and we are fooling ourselves (I John 1:8).

What does James 5:16 say?
Therefore confess your sins to each other and pray for each other so that you may be healed. The prayer of a righteous man is powerful and effective.

What does Matthew 5:23-24 say?
Therefore, if you are offering your gift at the altar and there remember that your brother has something against you, leave your gift there in front of the altar. First go and be reconciled to your brother; then come and offer your gift.

These suggest that confession to other people is important if we have sinned against them.
Sometimes we act as if no one knows our sin. Do you do that sometimes?

Read the following verses about people who think God does not see their sin.
Psalms 10:2, 11 In his arrogance the wicked man hunts down the weak, who are caught in the schemes he devises...He says to himself, "God has forgotten; he covers his face and never sees."

Psalms 64:2, 5 Hide me from the conspiracy of the wicked, from that noisy crowd of evildoers. They encourage each other in evil plans, they talk about hiding their snares; they say, "Who will see them ?"

Psalms 73:3, 11 For I envied the arrogant when I saw the prosperity of the wicked. They say, "How can God know? Does the Most High have knowledge?"

Psalms 94:7-11 They say, "The LORD does not see; the God of Jacob pays no heed." Take heed, you senseless ones among the people; you fools, when will you become wise? Does he who implanted the ear not hear? Does he who formed the eye not see? Does he who disciplines nations not punish? Does he who teaches man lack knowledge? The LORD knows the thoughts of man; he knows that they are futile.

Isaiah 29:15 Woe to those who go to great depths to hide their plans from the LORD, who do their work in darkness and think, "Who sees us? Who will know?"

But does God see our sin?
Proverbs 15:3 The eyes of the LORD are everywhere, keeping watch on the wicked and the good.
Read the following verses written by David, King of Israel. They talk about how he felt when he tried to hide his sin from God and from other people. (David's sin was committing adultery with Bathsheba and arranging to have her husband killed in battle.)

Psalms 32:3-5 When I kept silent, my bones wasted away through my groaning all day long. For day and night your hand was heavy upon me; my strength was sapped as in the heat of summer... Then I acknowledged my sin to you and did not cover up my iniquity. I said, "I will confess my transgressions to the LORD"— and you forgave the guilt of my sin.

Psalms 38:1-18 O LORD, do not rebuke me in your anger or discipline me in your wrath.
For your arrows have pierced me, and your hand has come down upon me. Because of your wrath there is no health in my body; my bones have no soundness because of my sin.
My guilt has overwhelmed me like a burden too heavy to bear.
My wounds fester and are loathsome because of my sinful folly.
I am bowed down and brought very low; all day long I go about mourning.
My back is filled with searing pain; there is no health in my body. I am feeble and utterly crushed;
I groan in anguish of heart.
All my longings lie open before you, O Lord; my sighing is not hidden from you.
My heart pounds, my strength fails me; even the light has gone from my eyes.
My friends and companions avoid me because of my wounds; my neighbors stay far away.
Those who seek my life set their traps, those who would harm me talk of my ruin;
all day long they plot deception.
I am like a deaf man, who cannot hear, like a mute, who cannot open his mouth;
I have become like a man who does not hear, whose mouth can offer no reply.
I wait for you, O LORD; you will answer, O Lord my God.
For I said, "Do not let them gloat or exalt themselves over me when my foot slips."
For I am about to fall, and my pain is ever with me.
I confess my iniquity; I am troubled by my sin.

Lesson 18. I don't want to tell someone about my sin. It's too embarrassing!

Did you know that Psalm 51 (where David confesses his sin) was written to the chief musician and sung before the whole congregation? Everyone heard about David's sin.

Psalm 32 (see earlier page) has the title Maschil which means it was to instruct others; so this too was not private.
Have you sinned against God and not told Him you did wrong?

Why not tell Him now?

Have you sinned against someone else?
Why not go to them and tell them you were wrong?

Are you forsaking your sin too? (forsaking means to leave it, stop doing it)

What kind of a person does God look to?
Isaiah 66:2 Has not my hand made all these things, and so they came into being?" declares the LORD. "This is the one I esteem: he who is humble and contrite in spirit, and trembles at my word."

Lesson 19. How do you feel about being corrected?

    Read Chapter 19. Choose a verse to share.
    Memorize 6:23.

How do you feel about being corrected?

Do you feel better than the person correcting you?
Then you are proud.

Do you feel the correction has nothing to do with you?
Then you may be a fool.

Do you dislike the person who corrects you?
Then you are a mocker.

Do you love the one correcting you, even if they are wrong?
Then you are wise.

Proverbs has a lot to say about being corrected. Proverbs uses the word <u>discipline</u> for correction. Sometimes the word <u>rebuke</u> is used, sometimes <u>advice</u>. The next page lists the Proverbs on correction or discipline.

Answer the following questions and give the verse or verses where you found your answer.

1. Are the corrections of discipline the way to life?

    (Then will you never be too old for discipline?)

2. What does a mocker think of discipline, correction or rebuke?

3. What does a fool think of being corrected by discipline, rebuke, or instruction?

4. What does a wise man think of being corrected?

Lesson 19. How do you feel about being corrected?

---

5. What happens to the person who despises, or hates, or refuses discipline?

6. Should we love to be corrected?

7. What is your feeling about being corrected?

Give example:

Proverbs on Correction

1:20-33 Wisdom calls aloud ... "How long will you simple ones love your simple ways? How long will mockers delight in mockery and fools hate knowledge?
If you had responded to my rebuke, I would have poured out my heart to you and made my thoughts known to you.
But since you rejected me when I called... I will mock when calamity overtakes you...
Since they would not accept my advice and spurned my rebuke, they will eat the fruit of their ways
But whoever listens to me will live in safety and be at ease, without fear of harm."

3:11,12 My son, do not despise the LORD's discipline and do not resent his rebuke, because the LORD disciplines those he loves, as a father the son he delights in.

5:7-13 Keep to a path far from her (the adulteress), lest...
at the end of your life you will groan
"How I hated discipline! How my heart spurned correction!
I would not obey my teachers or listen to my instructors."

6:23 ... the corrections of discipline are the way to life,

9:7, 8 "Whoever corrects a mocker invites insult; whoever rebukes a wicked man incurs abuse. Do not rebuke a mocker or he will hate you; rebuke a wise man and he will love you.

10:17 He who heeds discipline shows the way to life, but whoever ignores correction leads others astray.

12:1 Whoever loves discipline loves knowledge, but he who hates correction is stupid.

13:1 A wise son heeds his father's instruction, but a mocker does not listen to rebuke.

13:18 He who ignores discipline comes to poverty and shame, but whoever heeds correction is honored.

15:5 A fool spurns his father's discipline, but whoever heeds correction shows prudence.

15:10 Stern discipline awaits him who leaves the path; he who hates correction will die.

15:12 A mocker resents correction; he will not consult the wise.

15:31-33 He who listens to a life-giving rebuke will be at home among the wise.
He who ignores discipline despises himself, but whoever heeds correction gains understanding.
The fear of the LORD teaches a man wisdom, and humility comes before honor.

17:10 A rebuke impresses a man of discernment more than a hundred lashes a fool.

19:25 ...rebuke a discerning man, and he will gain knowledge.

29:1 A man who remains stiff-necked after many rebukes will suddenly be destroyed— without remedy.

29:15 The rod of correction imparts wisdom, but a child left to himself disgraces his mother.

Lesson 20. Do you ever think your way is right?

      Read chapter 20. Choose a verse to share.
      Memorize 16:2.

Do you ever think your way is right?

Take a look at the following proverbs
3:7 Do not be wise in your own eyes; fear the LORD and shun evil.

12:15 The way of a fool seems right to him, but a wise man listens to advice.

14:12 There is a way that seems right to a man, but in the end it leads to death.

16:2 All a man's ways seem innocent to him, but motives are weighed by the LORD.

21:2 All a man's ways seem right to him, but the LORD weighs the heart.

30:12 those who are pure in their own eyes and yet are not cleansed of their filth;

Isaiah 5:20-21 Woe to those who call evil good and good evil, who put darkness for light and light for darkness, who put bitter for sweet and sweet for bitter. Woe to those who are wise in their own eyes and clever in their own sight.

Do you think a person could believe something was right and actually be wrong?

Do you think you could do that?
Give an example.

What can happen to someone who ignores God's wisdom and decides to do whatever is right in his own eyes?

How can we know what is right?

Read also the following verses to find ways of knowing what is right.

1:1-7 The proverbs of Solomon son of David, king of Israel:
for attaining wisdom and discipline;
for understanding words of insight;
for acquiring a disciplined and prudent life, doing what is right and just and fair;
for giving prudence to the simple, knowledge and discretion to the young—
let the wise listen and add to their learning, and let the discerning get guidance—
for understanding proverbs and parables, the sayings and riddles of the wise.
The fear of the LORD is the beginning of knowledge, but fools despise wisdom and discipline.

Psalms 19:7-14 The law of the LORD is perfect, reviving the soul.
The statutes of the LORD are trustworthy, making wise the simple.
The precepts of the LORD are right, giving joy to the heart.
The commands of the LORD are radiant, giving light to the eyes.
The fear of the LORD is pure, enduring forever.
The ordinances of the LORD are sure and altogether righteous.
They are more precious than gold, than much pure gold;
they are sweeter than honey, than honey from the comb.
By them is your servant warned; in keeping them there is great reward.
Who can discern his errors? Forgive my hidden faults.
Keep your servant also from willful sins; may they not rule over me.
Then will I be blameless, innocent of great transgression.
May the words of my mouth and the meditation of my heart be pleasing in your sight, O LORD, my Rock and my Redeemer.

2:1-9 My son, if you accept my words and store up my commands within you,
turning your ear to wisdom and applying your heart to understanding,
and if you call out for insight and cry aloud for understanding,
and if you look for it as for silver and search for it as for hidden treasure,
then you will understand the fear of the LORD and find the knowledge of God.
For the LORD gives wisdom, and from his mouth come knowledge and understanding.
He holds victory in store for the upright, he is a shield to those whose walk is blameless,
for He guards the course of the just and protects the way of his faithful ones.
Then you will understand what is right and just and fair—every good path.

3:5-6 Trust in the LORD with all your heart and lean not on your own understanding; 6 in all your ways acknowledge him, and he will make your paths straight.

Psalms 119:9-11 How can a young man keep his way pure?
By living according to your word.
I seek you with all my heart; do not let me stray from your commands.
I have hidden your word in my heart that I might not sin against you.

2 Timothy 3:16-17 All Scripture is God-breathed and is useful for teaching, rebuking, correcting and training in righteousness, so that the man of God may be thoroughly equipped for every good work.

James 3:13-18 Who is wise and understanding among you?
Let him show it by his good life, by deeds done in the humility that comes from wisdom.
But if you harbor bitter envy and selfish ambition in your hearts,
do not boast about it or deny the truth.
Such "wisdom" does not come down from heaven but is earthly, unspiritual, of the devil.
For where you have envy and selfish ambition, there you find disorder and every evil practice.
But the wisdom that comes from heaven is first of all pure; then peace-loving, considerate,
submissive, full of mercy and good fruit, impartial and sincere.
Peacemakers who sow in peace raise a harvest of righteousness.

Father/leader: See the following examples where people did what they thought was right, but they were wrong.

1. Eve was tricked by the serpent (Genesis 3:13, I Timothy 2:14) into believing it was right to eat the fruit (Genesis 3:1-6).

2. Isaac believed it was right to pass his blessing to Esau (Genesis 27:1-4) even though God had said Esau was to serve Jacob (Genesis 25:23).

3. Rebecca, Isaac's wife, knew Jacob was supposed to receive the blessing, but believed she must trick her husband to see God's promise fulfilled. (Genesis 27:6-46)

Lesson 21. Would you like a lot of money? What would you do with it?

    Read chapter 21. Choose a verse to share.
    Memorize 23:4.

Would you like a lot of money?

What would you do with $250,000 if someone gave it to you?
    I would buy:
    I would give to:
    I would keep:

The verses on the next page are Proverbs about money or riches. Let's see what God's wisdom is on riches. Answer the following questions and give the verse where you found the answer.

What is better than riches or money?

What can happen from being greedy of gain (wanting much money)?

What does the book of Proverbs say about the person who wants to get rich quickly?

What do the following verses suggest *might* come with riches? (underline)

15:16 Better a little with the fear of the LORD than great wealth with turmoil.

21:6 A fortune made by a lying tongue is a fleeting vapor and a deadly snare.

22:16 He who oppresses the poor to increase his wealth and he who gives gifts to the rich—both come to poverty.

28:6 Better a poor man whose walk is blameless than a rich man whose ways are perverse.

28:11 A rich man may be wise in his own eyes, but a poor man who has discernment sees through him.

30:7-9 "Two things I ask of you, O LORD; do not refuse me before I die: 8 Keep falsehood and lies far from me; give me neither poverty nor riches, but give me only my daily bread. 9 Otherwise, I

Lesson 21. Would you like a lot of money? What would you do with it?

may have too much and disown you and say, 'Who is the LORD?' Or I may become poor and steal, and so dishonor the name of my God.

Remember that riches can be a blessing of wisdom:
Proverbs 3:16 Long life is in her [wisdom's] right hand; in her left hand are riches and honor.

It is the desire for riches or the love of money that causes trouble:
I Timothy 6:10 For the love of money is a root of all kinds of evil. Some people, eager for money, have wandered from the faith and pierced themselves with many griefs.

Whose wisdom is it to work with a goal of being rich?

What should we do with our money?

What happens if we try to keep our money to ourselves?

Do you still want a lot of money?

What will you do with your money now?

Proverbs on Riches

1:19 Such is the end of all who go after ill-gotten gain; it takes away the lives of those who get it.

3:9, 10 Honor the LORD with your wealth, with the first fruits of all your crops; then your barns will be filled to overflowing, and your vats will brim over with new wine.

3:14, 15 ...for [wisdom] is more profitable than silver and yields better returns than gold. She is more precious than rubies; nothing you desire can compare with her.

11:24, 25 One man gives freely, yet gains even more; another withholds unduly, but comes to poverty. A generous man will prosper; he who refreshes others will himself be refreshed.

13:7 One man pretends to be rich, yet has nothing; another pretends to be poor, yet has great wealth.

15:16 Better a little with the fear of the LORD than great wealth with turmoil.

15:27 A greedy man brings trouble to his family, but he who hates bribes will live.

19:17 He who is kind to the poor lends to the LORD, and he will reward him for what he has done.

21:6 A fortune made by a lying tongue is a fleeting vapor and a deadly snare.

22:1 A good name is more desirable than great riches; to be esteemed is better than silver or gold.

22:9 A generous man will himself be blessed, for he shares his food with the poor.

22:16 He who oppresses the poor to increase his wealth and he who gives gifts to the rich—both come to poverty.

23:4 Do not wear yourself out to get rich; have the wisdom to show restraint.

28:6 Better a poor man whose walk is blameless than a rich man whose ways are perverse.

28:11 A rich man may be wise in his own eyes, but a poor man who has discernment sees through him.

28:20 A faithful man will be richly blessed, but one eager to get rich will not go unpunished.

28:22 A stingy man is eager to get rich and is unaware that poverty awaits him.

28:27 He who gives to the poor will lack nothing, but he who closes his eyes to them receives many curses.

30:7-9 Two things I ask of you, O LORD; do not refuse me before I die:
Keep falsehood and lies far from me; give me neither poverty nor riches,
but give me only my daily bread.
Otherwise, I may have too much and disown you and say, "Who is the LORD ?"
Or I may become poor and steal, and so dishonor the name of my God.

Lesson 22. Are you proud? Of what?

    Read chapter 22. Choose a verse to share.
    Memorize 22:4.

Are you proud? Answer:

What are you proud of?

Below is a list of the Proverbs on pride and the opposite character—humility. Read them carefully.

3:34 He [God] mocks proud mockers but gives grace to the humble.

6:16, 17 There are six things the LORD hates, seven that are detestable to him: haughty eyes...

8:13 To fear the LORD is to hate evil; I hate pride and arrogance...

11:2 When pride comes, then comes disgrace, but with humility comes wisdom.

13:10 Pride only breeds quarrels, but wisdom is found in those who take advice.

18:12 Before his downfall a man's heart is proud, but humility comes before honor.

15:25 The LORD tears down the proud man's house but he keeps the widow's boundaries intact.

15:33 The fear of the LORD teaches a man wisdom, and humility comes before honor.

16:5 The LORD detests all the proud of heart.
    Be sure of this: They will not go unpunished.

16:18 Pride goes before destruction, a haughty spirit before a fall.

16:19 Better to be lowly in spirit and among the oppressed than to share plunder with the proud.

21:4 Haughty eyes and a proud heart, the lamp of the wicked, are sin!

22:4 Humility and the fear of the LORD bring wealth and honor and life.

21:24 The proud and arrogant man... "Mocker" is his name; he behaves with overweening pride.

29:23 A man's pride brings him low, but a man of lowly spirit gains honor.

Answer the following questions and give the reference of the verse or verses where you found the answer.

1. What does God think about pride?

2. What should you think about pride?

3. What comes from being proud?

4. What comes from being humble?

5. What is a clue that you or someone else is proud?

Pride can be sneaky. One moment we may just be happy about what we did or what we have. The next moment we may become proud.

7. Why is humility or a contrite spirit so important if we want God's help?
   Proverbs 3:34 He mocks proud mockers but gives grace to the humble.

   Isaiah 66:2 Has not my hand made all these things, and so they came into being?" declares the LORD. "This is the one I esteem: he who is humble and contrite in spirit, and trembles at my word.

8. Do you want to be humble?

One way to turn pride into humility is to thank God from your heart for the thing you are proud of. Praise Him and take no credit for yourself.

9. Give an example of when you were proud.

10. Give an example of when you were humble.

Lesson 23. The fear of the Lord. Why is it so important?

    Read chapter 23 and choose a verse to share.
    Memorize 1:7 and 9:10.

The "fear of the Lord." Proverbs seems to think it is pretty important. Why is it important? What is it anyway?

Let's look at what Proverbs says about the fear of the Lord. Maybe then we will see why it is important and maybe what it is.

Proverbs on the fear of the Lord

1:7 The fear of the LORD is the beginning of knowledge, but fools despise wisdom and discipline.

1:29 Since they hated knowledge and did not choose to fear the LORD,

2:5 then you will understand the fear of the LORD and find the knowledge of God.

3:7 Do not be wise in your own eyes; fear the LORD and shun evil.

8:13 To fear the LORD is to hate evil; I hate pride and arrogance, evil behavior and perverse speech.

9:10 The fear of the LORD is the beginning of wisdom, and knowledge of the Holy One is understanding.

10:27 The fear of the LORD adds length to life, but the years of the wicked are cut short.

14:26 He who fears the LORD has a secure fortress, and for his children it will be a refuge.

14:27 The fear of the LORD is a fountain of life, turning a man from the snares of death.

15:16 Better a little with the fear of the LORD than great wealth with turmoil.

15:33 The fear of the LORD teaches a man wisdom, and humility comes before honor.

16:6 Through love and faithfulness sin is atoned for; through the fear of the LORD a man avoids evil.

19:23 The fear of the LORD leads to life: Then one rests content, untouched by trouble.

22:4 Humility and the fear of the LORD bring wealth and honor and life.

Lesson 23. The fear of the Lord. Why is it so important?

23:17 Do not let your heart envy sinners, but always be zealous for the fear of the LORD.

24:21 Fear the LORD and the king, my son, and do not join with the rebellious,

Answer the following questions, giving the verse where you found the answer.

1. What is the beginning of knowledge and wisdom?

2. Can we get knowledge and wisdom (the spiritual kind) without having the fear of the Lord?

3. Can we understand the fear of the Lord without wanting to obey?

    What does 2:1-5 say? **My son, if you accept my words and store up my commands within you, turning your ear to wisdom and applying your heart to understanding, and if you call out for insight and cry aloud for understanding, and if you look for it as for silver and search for it as for hidden treasure, then you will understand the fear of the LORD and find the knowledge of God.**

4. What attitude or feeling must we have to understand the fear of the Lord? (2:1-5)

5. If you fear the Lord, will you be satisfied?

6. Are you satisfied?
   Then are you fearing the Lord?

7. If you fear the Lord, what will you do?

8. Are you doing these things?

9. What are the blessings of fearing the Lord?

10. What is better than money with turmoil?

11. The fear of the Lord seems to be that we want to obey the Lord before we know what we are to obey.

    It is more than obeying the Lord. It means you have so much respect and trust in God that you want to obey Him no matter what He asks you to do.
    What does the verse below reveal about *fearing* God versus *being afraid* of God?

Exodus 20:10 Moses said to the people, "Do not be afraid. God has come to test you, so that the fear of God will be with you to keep you from sinning."

What do these verses say?
Psalms 119:120 [David speaking] My flesh trembles in fear of you; I stand in awe of your laws.

Psalms 130:3-4 If you, O LORD, kept a record of sins, O Lord, who could stand? But with you there is forgiveness; therefore you are feared.

12. Do you fear the Lord?
    Give an example of when you feared the Lord.
    (In other words, a time when you did something right simply because you feared God.)

13. Give an example of when you did not fear the Lord.
    (In other words, when you did something bad because you chose to ignore God.)

14. Read Psalms 34:9-14. What does it tell us?
    Fear the LORD, you his saints, for those who fear him lack nothing.
    The lions may grow weak and hungry, but those who seek the LORD lack no good thing.
    Come, my children, listen to me; I will teach you the fear of the LORD.
    Whoever of you loves life and desires to see many good days, keep your tongue from evil and your lips from speaking lies.
    Turn from evil and do good; seek peace and pursue it.

15. How do you get the fear of the Lord? *(give your opinion)*

16. Are you going to fear the Lord?

Lesson 24. Are you lazy?

> Read chapter 24 and share a verse.
> Memorize 13:4.

Are you lazy? Or do you work hard and use your time carefully? If you are lazy, you are <u>slothful</u> or a <u>sluggard</u> according to Proverbs. This lesson will be on that subject. The next lesson will be on the diligent (hard-working) person. Remember that the proverbs are not given to make us feel bad about ourselves, but to help us learn how to please God and lead a good life.

Below is a list of the Proverbs on slothfulness and diligence. Study them carefully.

Verses on diligence and slothfulness (laziness)

6:6-11 Go to the ant, you sluggard; consider its ways and be wise!
It has no commander, no overseer or ruler,
yet it stores its provisions in summer and gathers its food at harvest.
How long will you lie there, you sluggard? When will you get up from your sleep?
A little sleep, a little slumber, a little folding of the hands to rest-
and poverty will come on you like a bandit and scarcity like an armed man.

10:4 Lazy hands make a man poor, but diligent hands bring wealth.

10:5 He who gathers crops in summer is a wise son, but he who sleeps during harvest is a disgraceful son.

10:26 As vinegar to the teeth and smoke to the eyes, so is a sluggard to those who send him.

12:24 Diligent hands will rule, but laziness ends in slave labor.

12:27 The lazy man does not roast his game, but the diligent man prizes his possessions.

13:4 The sluggard craves and gets nothing, but the desires of the diligent are fully satisfied.

15:19 The way of the sluggard is blocked with thorns, but the path of the upright is a highway.

18:9 One who is slack in his work is brother to one who destroys.

19:15 Laziness brings on deep sleep, and the shiftless man goes hungry.

19:24 The sluggard buries his hand in the dish; he will not even bring it back to his mouth!

20:4 A sluggard does not plow in season; so at harvest time he looks but finds nothing.

20:13 Do not love sleep or you will grow poor; stay awake and you will have food to spare.

21:5 The plans of the diligent lead to profit as surely as haste leads to poverty.

21:25 The sluggard's craving will be the death of him, because his hands refuse to work.

22:13 The sluggard says, "There is a lion outside!" or, "I will be murdered in the streets!"

22:29 Do you see a man skilled in his work?
He will serve before kings; he will not serve before obscure men.

24:30-34 I went past the field of the sluggard, past the vineyard of the man who lacks judgment; thorns had come up everywhere, the ground was covered with weeds, and the stone wall was in ruins.
I applied my heart to what I observed and learned a lesson from what I saw:
A little sleep, a little slumber, a little folding of the hands to rest-and poverty will come on you like a bandit and scarcity like an armed man.

26:13 The sluggard says, "There is a lion in the road, a fierce lion roaming the streets!"

26:14 As a door turns on its hinges, so a sluggard turns on his bed.

26:15 The sluggard buries his hand in the dish; he is too lazy to bring it back to his mouth.

26:16 The sluggard is wiser in his own eyes than seven men who answer discreetly.

Answer the following questions and give the reference of the verse where you found your answer. Does the sluggard get what he wants?

1. Why not?

2. Does the slothful person, or sluggard, like to sleep a lot?

3. Do you like to sleep a lot?

4. Is the slothful person poor?

5. Is he a good worker, someone to depend upon?

    Are you?

Lesson 24. Are you lazy?

6. Does he work when it is time to work?

7. What excuses does he give for not working?

8. Does he think he is right?

9. Are you ever slothful?

10. What does an unwatched vineyard teach about the slothful?

11. What does Proverb 21:5 say about rushing through your work?

12. What do 12:27 and 18:9 say about wasting things?

13. Give an example of when you were slothful.

14. If you fear the Lord, what will you think about slothfulness in your life

15. If you are a fool, what will you think of being lazy?

16. If you are a mocker, what will you think of being lazy?

17. What do <u>you</u> think of being lazy now?

Lesson 25. Would you like to be diligent?

>Read chapter 25 and choose a verse to share.
>Memorize Proverbs 12:24.

After the lesson on slothfulness, would you like to be the opposite...diligent? Diligent means that you work hard at the right time and use your time carefully.

Review the list of Proverbs on diligence and slothfulness from Lesson 24 and answer the following questions, giving the reference.

1. What example does the ant give for being diligent?

2. Does the diligent work when it is time to work?

3. Does the diligent take care of his belongings?

4. Would the diligent make a good leader?

5. Is the diligent poor?

6. Do you work hard when you work? Give an example.

7. Do you work when it's time to work?
   Do you offer to help only when there is no work to do? Give an example.

8. Are you careful with what you have?
   Give an example.

9. Do you use your time carefully?
   Give an example.

Some people work "hard all the time."
They work many more hours than others, but don't seem to get things done.
Are they diligent, or not?

Lesson 26. How can parents help their children?

Read chapter 26. Choose a verse to share.
Memorize Proverbs 13:24.

How can parents help their children?

They can teach them wisdom.

This builds wise, godly character which will result in godly conduct and be a blessing throughout their life.

Helping your children find wisdom is more valuable than giving them straight teeth, material advantages, good education, social opportunities, an I-pad, etc... *(Review Chapter 6 for the blessings of wisdom)*

Let's see how Proverbs shows parents how to help their children.

Proverbs and Children

3:12 ...because the LORD disciplines those he loves, as a father the son he delights in.

13:24 He who spares the rod hates his son, but he who loves him is careful to discipline him.

19:18 Discipline your son, for in that there is hope; do not be a willing party to his death.

22:6 Train up a child in the way he should go, and when he is old he will not turn from it.

22:15 Folly is bound up in the heart of a child, but the rod of discipline will drive it far from him.

23:13, 14 Do not withhold discipline from a child; if you punish him with the rod, he will not die. Punish him with the rod and save his soul from death.

29:15 The rod of correction imparts wisdom, but a child left to himself disgraces his mother.

29:17 Discipline your son, and he will give you peace; he will bring delight to your soul.

Reread Proverbs 3:12 and 13:24. Why should parents correct their children?

What will a parent do for his child if he loves him?

What will a parent do for his child if he hates him?

Does Proverbs promise wisdom for children if they are corrected in anger by the parent?

Read 13:24 and 23:13, 14. Does chastening include physical discipline (spanking*) or just verbal discipline (lectures) and restriction of privileges (go to room, no TV, etc)?

Note on spanking: a non-personal, hard object like a rod should be used, not your hand (personal) which is used to reach out in love. Afterward, reassure your child of your love for him.

Read 22:15. Is a child naturally foolish, or naturally wise?
    What will drive out the foolishness?
    Will anything else (example—verbal lecture) drive it out?

Read 29:15. What besides a rod will give wisdom?

Will God bless loving correction of a child? (Read 29:17, 22:6)
    How?

Will the child like the discipline?

Should you stop the discipline if the child cries?

Should you avoid discipline if the child cries loudly whenever disciplined?

What happens if parents don't discipline their children? (29:15, 23:13-14)

NOTE: Disciplining children wisely faces most parents with their own personal challenge — the need to develop their own self-control. The motive for wise discipline is love and delight (13:24; 3:12). When anger is the motive for discipline, whether with a rod or with words, the discipline is not wise but foolish. In this case the parent communicates rejection of the child and the result is not the building of wisdom in the child. Instead the child learns that lashing out physically or in harsh words when angry is the way to be if you have power.

Those who oppose using the rod these days because they believe this wisdom to be "barbaric", but instead use words out of anger, damage the child in the same way that using the rod out of anger damages the child – both drive the child towards mockery or folly because of the personal rejection. Thus, parents need to develop their own self-control to discipline wisely. Parents who find themselves overwhelmed with the day to day pressures of an intensely busy life (for example, over scheduling of events and instant communication demands of electronic devices) may need to find ways to simplify their lives in order to work on developing their own self-control.

Lesson 26. How can parents help their children?

How can parents know when to use the rod and when to use instruction when correcting their children?

The answer depends on whether the child needs correction because he acted like a simple person, a mocker, or a fool. The simple child needs instruction. The mocker and foolish child need the rod. *See the next two pages for a discussion of this.*

Parents   Give examples of a time when you wisely corrected your child and a time when you unwisely corrected your child.

Children   Give an example of when you thought you were wisely corrected or punished by your parents.

Give an example of a time when you think you should have been corrected, but were not.

Give an example of when you were corrected wrongly (in your opinion) by your parents.

Parents: While the following material may be too complicated for some of your children to understand, it is important to share these principles of discipline with them so they know the rules of engagement ahead of time.

Discernment in discipline

We can learn from Proverbs the different types of personality traits, match them with our children's behavior, and use the corresponding methods of instruction given in Proverbs.

Notice the different characteristics of a fool, a simple, and a mocker in Proverbs.

A <u>simple</u> person is not prudent (14:15,18; 22:3)
    apparently looks up to the mocker (21:11; 19:25)
    does not foresee evil or the consequences of his actions (22:3)
    loves his simplicity (1:22)
    is gullible (14:15)
    and therefore folly just naturally falls on him (14:18)

When your child acts like a simple person, the way to make him wise and prudent is through teaching him the wisdom of Proverbs. The implications are that he will respond to the teaching. He mainly needs encouragement and instruction. He may often get into serious disobedience as a result of his lack of prudence and gullibility, but the response for correction is mainly teaching rather than physical discipline. The simple person needs the wisdom of Proverbs (1:1, 4; 8:5; 9:4), and instruction in right behavior.

A <u>mocker</u> delights in his mocking (1:22)
> is mocked by God (3:34)
> cannot handle correction in his life (9:7,8; 15:12;13:1; 19:28)
> seeks after wisdom, but cannot find it (14:6)
>> because he has bypassed the fear of the lord (9:10)
> refuses to go to the wise for wisdom (15:12)
> creates contention (22:10)
>> and therefore is proud (13:10)
>> and will have difficulty getting along with others (24:9)

If your child is a mocker or disobeys at times because he has mocked your instruction (in contrast to being a simple person) the general response is physical discipline (22:10) rather than instruction (which he scorns) although wisdom cries out to the mocker in rebuke (1:22, 23).

Note: it may be common practice in your home to come down hard on your child who through simplicity has committed serious disobedience. At the same time the mocker is simply scolded for a mocking attitude as long as there is no "serious" misbehavior. Proverbs indicates the opposite should be true. The severity of our chastening tends, in our wisdom, to be proportional to the potential or actual consequences of the disobedience. Proverbs indicates that the severity and <u>type</u> of chastening should correspond to the characteristic motivating the child in his disobedience. Mocking attitudes appear to deserve far greater chastening than may be the case in our homes.

A <u>fool</u> despises wisdom and instruction (1:7; 15:5; 17:16; 23:9)

> hates knowledge (1:22)
> does not want understanding (18:2)
> is a sorrow to his parents (10:1; 15:20; 17:21,25; 19:13)
> has no wisdom (10:21; 16:22; 24:7)
> may be mischievous (10:23)
> thinks he is right (12:15)
> is hasty to wrath (12:16; 14:17; 27:3)
> speaks foolishly (12:23; 15:2) rather than wisely (15:7; 17:7;29:11)
> thinks it is abomination to depart from evil (13:19; 14:9,16)
> is proud (14:3) and thus enters into contention (13:10; 18:6)
> feeds on foolishness (15:14)
> is not dependable (26:6)
> goes back to his folly though detestable (26:11)
> and is not due honor (26:1,8).

If your child has the characteristics of a fool or disobeys due to his foolishness as described above, physical discipline should definitely be applied while he is a child (22:15), for otherwise, it may do little good (17:10; 27:22) even though it is his due (19:29; 26:3).

> "Folly is bound up in the heart of a child,
> but the rod of discipline will drive it far from him."(22:15)

Some clues to help identify these different characteristics are:

<u>simple</u>
      naive, gullible
      forgetful
      careless
      follows others into trouble
      impulsive

<u>mocker</u>
      talks back
      argues
      stubbornness

<u>fool</u>
      doesn't listen
      intent on his own way and desires
      demanding
      angry
      gets into mischief on purpose to get attention

Lesson 27. Should I choose my friends? How?

      Read chapter 27 and choose a verse to share.
      Memorize Proverbs 22:24-25.

Do you choose your friends? How?

Proverbs teaches that we are to choose our friends. But the way we choose them, according to Proverbs, may be quite different than what we think.

The following areas show God's wisdom on this matter. Let's see what they say.

Proverbs and Friends

13:20 He who walks with the wise grows wise, but a companion of fools suffers harm.

14:7 Stay away from a foolish man, for you will not find knowledge on his lips.

18:24 A man of many companions may come to ruin, but there is a friend who sticks closer than a brother.

22:24-25 Do not make friends with a hot-tempered man, do not associate with one easily angered, or you may learn his ways and get yourself ensnared.

24:21, 22 Fear the LORD and the king, my son, and do not join with the rebellious, for those two will send sudden destruction upon them, and who knows what calamities they can bring?

27:9 Perfume and incense bring joy to the heart, and the pleasantness of one's friend springs from his earnest counsel.

27:17 As iron sharpens iron, so one man sharpens another.

28:7 He who keeps the law is a discerning son, but a companion of gluttons disgraces his father.

Lesson 27. Should I choose my friends? How?

Give references as you answer the questions below:

1. What kinds of people are we <u>not</u> to be close friends with?

2. Why should we not be friends with a fool?

   How can you tell if someone is a fool?
   (You may want to review Lesson 17 on the fool)

3. Why should we not be friends with an angry or furious man?

4. Why should we not spend time with people that are rebellious?

5. If we are not to be friends with certain people, does that mean we are to be unfriendly to them?
   1 Peter 2:17 Show proper respect to everyone: Love the brotherhood of believers, fear God, honor the king.

   Matthew 5:44-45 But I tell you: Love your enemies and pray for those who persecute you, that you may be sons of your Father in heaven. He causes his sun to rise on the evil and the good, and sends rain on the righteous and the unrighteous.

6. What do you think is the difference between loving these people and yet not being their friend?

7. What kind of people are we to have as friends?

8. How can you tell if someone is wise? (Proverbs 9:8)
   Do not rebuke a mocker or he will hate you; rebuke a wise man and he will love you.

9. Why are <u>wise</u> friends important to have?

10. To have friends are we to be friendly and loyal?

11. What happens to you if you have <u>no</u> friends?

Lesson 28. What is a leader?

Read chapter 28. Choose a verse to share.
Memorize Proverbs 3:3-4.

What is a leader?

Maybe sometimes we think of a leader as someone who is good at bossing people around.

This lesson is about the qualities of a leader who leads by being a good example.
By the way he lives, he stands ahead in his character, and by his good life, he shows others the way to wise character. Jesus Christ was that kind of leader.

Let's see the character of this kind of leader.

Read the references below and look for clues which would make a good character for a leader.
List the character traits and be ready to explain how a leader would act in this way.
The first question is answered as an example.

<u>Advice for a good leader: things that make a good leader.</u>

1. **3:3-4; 13:15 Let love and faithfulness never leave you; bind them around your neck, write them on the tablet of your heart. Then you will win favor and a good name in the sight of God and man**
   13:15 Good understanding wins favor, but the way of the unfaithful is hard.

   love, faithfulness: This means that he will show kindness along with truth to others and be understanding of their difficulties, joys, etc...

2. **3:27 Do not withhold good from those who deserve it, when it is in your power to act.**

3. **3:31 Do not envy a violent man or choose any of his ways.**

4. **10:12 Hatred stirs up dissension, but love covers over all wrongs.**

5. **11:3 The integrity of the upright guides them, but the unfaithful are destroyed by their duplicity.**

6. **12:15 The way of a fool seems right to him, but a wise man listens to advice.**
   19:20 Listen to advice and accept instruction, and in the end you will be wise.

Lesson 28. What is a leader?

20:5 The purposes of a man's heart are deep waters, but a man of understanding draws them out.

7. 12:24 Diligent hands will rule, but laziness ends in slave labor.

8. 13:10 Pride only breeds quarrels, but wisdom is found in those who take advice.
   3:34 He [God] mocks proud mockers but gives grace to the humble.

9. 14:17 A quick-tempered man does foolish things, and a crafty man is hated.
   14:29 A patient man has great understanding, but a quick-tempered man displays folly.
   19:11 A man's wisdom gives him patience; it is to his glory to overlook an offense.
   15:18 A hot-tempered man stirs up dissension, but a patient man calms a quarrel.
   29:22 An angry man stirs up dissension, and a hot-tempered one commits many sins.
   16:32 Better a patient man than a warrior,
      a man who controls his temper than one who takes a city.

10. 10:19 When words are many, sin is not absent, but he who holds his tongue is wise.
    11:13 A gossip betrays a confidence, but a trustworthy man keeps a secret.
    17:27 A man of knowledge uses words with restraint, and a man of understanding is
       even-tempered.
    21:23 He who guards his mouth and his tongue keeps himself from calamity.
    10:21 The lips of the righteous nourish many, but fools die for lack of judgment.
    10:31 The mouth of the righteous brings forth wisdom, but a perverse tongue will be cut out.
    15:7 The lips of the wise spread knowledge; not so the hearts of fools.
    15:23 A man finds joy in giving an apt reply— and how good is a timely word!

11. 17:7 Arrogant lips are unsuited to a fool— how much worse lying lips to a ruler!

12. 18:13 He who answers before listening— that is his folly and his shame.

13. 19:2 It is not good to have zeal without knowledge, nor to be hasty and miss the way.

14. 22:3 A prudent man sees danger and takes refuge, but the simple keep going and suffer for it.
    27:12 The prudent see danger and take refuge, but the simple keep going and suffer for it.

15. 24:23-25 These also are sayings of the wise: To show partiality in judging is not good: Whoever says to the guilty, "You are innocent"— peoples will curse him and nations denounce him. But it will go well with those who convict the guilty, and rich blessing will come upon them.

16. 27:2 Let another praise you, and not your own mouth; someone else, and not your own lips.

17. 24:21, 22 Fear the LORD and the king, my son, and do not join with the rebellious, for those two [LORD and king] will send sudden destruction upon them [rebellious], and who knows what calamities they can bring?

18. 31:3-5 Do not spend your strength on women, your vigor on those who ruin kings. "It is not for kings, O Lemuel— not for kings to drink wine, not for rulers to crave beer, lest they drink and forget what the law decrees, and deprive all the oppressed of their rights."

19. 18:14 A man's spirit sustains him in sickness, but a crushed spirit who can bear?

Father/leader: summarize the list above for your family.

The list showing the basic characteristics of this leader is long. It is not at all complete, for we could list almost all of Proverbs.

The list looks hard. But if we fear the Lord, this is the kind of character that God will begin to develop in us. We need to ask God for strength from the Holy Spirit.

Do you want that kind of character?

Do you want to be that kind of leader?

You can be this kind of leader if you are an adult or a child a girl or a boy, man or woman.

Read 2 Chronicles 16:9:
For the eyes of the LORD range throughout the earth to strengthen those whose hearts are fully committed to him.

God is looking all over for someone who wants wise character.

Lesson 29. For men and boys: dangers of the adulteress

Read chapter 29 and choose a verse to share.
Memorize Proverbs 7:24-27.

Proverbs has a lot to say about the adulteress, or immoral woman, which are the words used in the NIV. The three longest sections of Proverbs talk about the adulteress (5:3-21; 6:24-35; 7:24-27). The only subjects talked about more in Proverbs are the fool and the tongue. There are more warnings about the adulteress than about pride, or trying to be rich or scorning, or laziness. God, who had Solomon write these Proverbs, must think the dangers of the adulteress are very important to see.

What is an adulteress?

She is a woman who wants a man to come and make love, but she is not married to him. She is not the partner God has given him. Someone whom you know very well could be an adulteress. She may be a prostitute, a neighborhood wife, someone at work or someone in church. It all depends upon what she wants from the man who is not her husband.

This lesson explains the dangers of the adulteress to men and teenage (or pre-teen) boys. Women today can and often do act "like" the adulteress <u>without knowing it</u>, so even though this lesson is aimed at men and boys, the women and girls should complete it also.

<u>For men and boys: danger!</u>

<u>Read 2:10-19</u>
10 For wisdom will enter your heart, and knowledge will be pleasant to your soul. **11** Discretion will protect you, and understanding will guard you. **12** Wisdom will save you from the ways of wicked men, from men whose words are perverse, **13** who leave the straight paths to walk in dark ways, **14** who delight in doing wrong and rejoice in the perverseness of evil, **15** whose paths are crooked and who are devious in their ways.
16 It will save you also from the adulteress, from the wayward wife with her seductive words, **17** who has left the partner of her youth and ignored the covenant she made before God. **18** For her house leads down to death and her paths to the spirits of the dead. **19** None who go to her return or attain the paths of life.

<u>5:1-23</u>
1 My son, pay attention to my wisdom, listen well to my words of insight, **2** that you may maintain discretion and your lips may preserve knowledge. **3** For the lips of an adulteress drip honey, and her speech is smoother than oil; **4** but in the end she is bitter as gall, sharp as a double-edged sword. **5** Her feet go down to death; her steps lead straight to the grave. **6** She gives no thought to the way of life; her paths are crooked, but she knows it not.

7 Now then, my sons, listen to me; do not turn aside from what I say. **8** Keep to a path far from her, do not go near the door of her house, **9** lest you give your best strength to others and your years to one who is cruel, **10** lest strangers feast on your wealth and your toil enrich another man's house. **11** At the end of your life you will groan, when your flesh and body are spent. **12** You will say, "How I hated discipline! How my heart spurned correction! **13** I would not obey my teachers or listen to my instructors. **14** I have come to the brink of utter ruin in the midst of the whole assembly.
" **15** Drink water from your own cistern, running water from your own well. **16** Should your springs overflow in the streets, your streams of water in the public squares? **17** Let them be yours alone, never to be shared with strangers. **18** May your fountain be blessed, and may you rejoice in the wife of your youth. **19** A loving doe, a graceful deer— may her breasts satisfy you always, may you ever be captivated by her love.
20 Why be captivated, my son, by an adulteress? Why embrace the bosom of another man's wife? **21** For a man's ways are in full view of the LORD, and he examines all his paths. **22** The evil deeds of a wicked man ensnare him; the cords of his sin hold him fast. **23** He will die for lack of discipline, led astray by his own great folly.

6:20-35
20 My son, keep your father's commands and do not forsake your mother's teaching. **21** Bind them upon your heart forever; fasten them around your neck. **22** When you walk, they will guide you; when you sleep, they will watch over you; when you awake, they will speak to you. **23** For these commands are a lamp, this teaching is a light, and the corrections of discipline are the way to life, **24** keeping you from the immoral woman, from the smooth tongue of the wayward wife. **25** Do not lust in your heart after her beauty or let her captivate you with her eyes, **26** for the prostitute reduces you to a loaf of bread, and the adulteress preys upon your very life.
27 Can a man scoop fire into his lap without his clothes being burned? **28** Can a man walk on hot coals without his feet being scorched? **29** So is he who sleeps with another man's wife; no one who touches her will go unpunished. **30** Men do not despise a thief if he steals to satisfy his hunger when he is starving. **31** Yet if he is caught, he must pay sevenfold, though it costs him all the wealth of his house. **32** But a man who commits adultery lacks judgment; whoever does so destroys himself. **33** Blows and disgrace are his lot, and his shame will never be wiped away; **34** for jealousy arouses a husband's fury, and he will show no mercy when he takes revenge. **35** He will not accept any compensation; he will refuse the bribe, however great it is.

7:1-27
1 My son, keep my words and store up my commands within you. **2** Keep my commands and you will live; guard my teachings as the apple of your eye. **3** Bind them on your fingers; write them on the tablet of your heart. **4** Say to wisdom, "You are my sister," and call understanding your kinsman; **5** they will keep you from the adulteress, from the wayward wife with her seductive words.
6 At the window of my house I looked out through the lattice. **7** I saw among the simple, I noticed among the young men, a youth who lacked judgment. **8** He was going down the street near her corner, walking along in the direction of her house **9** at twilight, as the day was fading, as the dark of night set in. **10** Then out came a woman to meet him, dressed like a prostitute and with crafty intent. **11** (She is loud and defiant, her feet never stay at home; **12** now in the street, now in the squares, at every corner she lurks.) **13** She took hold of him and kissed him and with a brazen face she said: **14** "I have fellowship offerings at home; today I fulfilled my vows. **15** So I came out to meet you; I looked for you and have found you! **16** I have covered my bed with colored linens from Egypt. **17** I have

perfumed my bed with myrrh, aloes and cinnamon. **18** Come, let's drink deep of love till morning; let's enjoy ourselves with love! **19** My husband is not at home; he has gone on a long journey.
20 He took his purse filled with money and will not be home till full moon." **21** With persuasive words she led him astray; she seduced him with her smooth talk. **22** All at once he followed her like an ox going to the slaughter, like a deer stepping into a noose **23** till an arrow pierces his liver, like a bird darting into a snare, little knowing it will cost him his life. **24** Now then, my sons, listen to me; pay attention to what I say. **25** Do not let your heart turn to her ways or stray into her paths. **26** Many are the victims she has brought down; her slain are a mighty throng. **27** Her house is a highway to the grave, leading down to the chambers of death.

<u>23:26-28</u>
26 My son, give me your heart and let your eyes keep to my ways, **27** for a prostitute is a deep pit and a wayward wife is a narrow well. **28** Like a bandit she lies in wait, and multiplies the unfaithful among men.

<u>30:20</u>
20 "This is the way of an adulteress: She eats and wipes her mouth and says, 'I've done nothing wrong.'

Where might one run into an adulteress?
    2:17

    6:29

    7:10, 12

What are the ways the adulteress uses to attract a man?
    2:16

    5:3

    6:24, 25

    7:10

    7:15

    7:21

What other characteristics might she have?
    7:11

    7:13

    23:26-28

Does the adulteress believe she is doing anything wrong?
  5:6

  30:20

What might she do to keep a man from realizing the danger?
  7:21

Is the adulteress a danger for the young man?
  7:7-10

Is the adulteress a danger for the older, more mature man?
  7:26

What are the results of falling to the adulteress?
  2:19

  5:4

  5:9-11

  6:26-28

  6:32

  6:33

  7:22, 23

  7:27

What is the protection from the adulteress?
  2:10, 11, 16

  5:7, 8

  5:15, 17-19 (if you are married)

  6:23, 24

  7:24, 25

What is the adulteress *really* after, (though she may not be aware of this)?
  6:36

  7:21-23

Lesson 29. For men and boys: dangers of the adulteress

A good illustration of a strong man "slain" by an adulteress is David, king of Israel. He had walked with the Lord for years, trusting Him for his many fears and enemies. David was a very strong man. Yet he was overwhelmed by his desire for Bathsheba, the mother of Solomon who wrote these Proverbs on adulteress (2 Samuel 11:2-5).

David's adultery resulted in Bathsheba's pregnancy and David finally caused the murder of her husband. In chastisement the Lord took the life of the child (2 Samuel 12:14-18), and declared that the sword would never depart from David's house, that He would raise up evil against David out of his own house, would take his wives before his eyes, and would give them to his neighbor (2 Samuel 12:10, 11).

The consequences were devastating!
Many men and young men become involved with the adulteress without realizing what is happening. The men and young men think that the woman is really interested in them (flattery, ego-building). With their inflated egos and her eyelids flashing, they take the bait and are consumed. They would never have thought she was an "adulteress" until too late.

Involvement with the adulteress can ruin marriages, ministries, reputations, a young man's future, fellowship with God, and even bring death.

! DANGER !

Are you interested in knowing more about the adulteress?
Romans 16:19 Everyone has heard about your obedience, so I am full of joy over you; but I want you to be wise about what is good, and innocent about what is evil.

How should a man or boy treat girls and women when he is not married to them?

1 Timothy 5:2 [Treat] older women as mothers, and younger women as sisters, with absolute purity.

Lesson 30. The Virtuous Woman

Read Proverbs chapters 30-31 and share a verse.
Memorize 31:10.

Proverbs has much to say about the character of the woman of great value—the virtuous woman. Her value, according to God's wisdom, is far above rubies or precious jewels (31:10).

Proverbs also speaks about the unwise character in some women. Let's look at both. Underline the words showing good character in the following verses and circle the words showing bad character.

The virtuous woman
11:16 A kindhearted woman gains respect, but ruthless men gain only wealth.

12:4 A wife of noble character is her husband's crown, but a disgraceful wife is like decay in his bones.

14:1 The wise woman builds her house, but with her own hands the foolish one tears hers down.

19:14 Houses and wealth are inherited from parents, but a prudent wife is from the LORD.

31:10 A wife of noble character who can find? She is worth far more than rubies.

31:30 Charm is deceptive, and beauty is fleeting; but a woman who fears the LORD is to be praised.

The not-so-virtuous woman
11:22 Like a gold ring in a pig's snout is a beautiful woman who shows no discretion.

14:1 The wise woman builds her house, but with her own hands the foolish one tears hers down.

19:13 A foolish son is his father's ruin, and a quarrelsome wife is like a constant dripping.

21:9 Better to live on a corner of the roof than share a house with a quarrelsome wife.

21:19 Better to live in a desert than with a quarrelsome and ill-tempered wife.

25:24 Better to live on a corner of the roof than share a house with a quarrelsome wife.

27:15-16 A quarrelsome wife is like a constant dripping on a rainy day; restraining her is like restraining the wind or grasping oil with the hand.

30:20 "This is the way of an adulteress: She eats and wipes her mouth and says, 'I've done nothing wrong.'

If you are a woman or a girl, what kind of a woman should you try to be like?

What are the character traits of the not-so-virtuous woman?

If you are a boy or unmarried man, what character traits should you look for in a future wife?

Read the following description of the virtuous woman, and then answer the questions below.

Proverbs 31:10-31
A wife of noble character who can find? She is worth far more than rubies.
Her husband has full confidence in her and lacks nothing of value.
She brings him good, not harm, all the days of her life.
She selects wool and flax and works with eager hands.
She is like the merchant ships, bringing her food from afar.
She gets up while it is still dark;
she provides food for her family and portions for her servant girls.
She considers a field and buys it; out of her earnings she plants a vineyard.
She sets about her work vigorously; her arms are strong for her tasks.
She sees that her trading is profitable, and her lamp does not go out at night.
In her hand she holds the distaff and grasps the spindle with her fingers.
She opens her arms to the poor and extends her hands to the needy.
When it snows, she has no fear for her household; for all of them are clothed in scarlet.
She makes coverings for her bed; she is clothed in fine linen and purple.
Her husband is respected at the city gate,
here he takes his seat among the elders of the land.
She makes linen garments and sells them, and supplies the merchants with sashes.
She is clothed with strength and dignity; she can laugh at the days to come.
She speaks with wisdom, and faithful instruction is on her tongue.
She watches over the affairs of her household and does not eat the bread of idleness.
Her children arise and call her blessed; her husband also, and he praises her:
"Many women do noble things, but you surpass them all."
Charm is deceptive, and beauty is fleeting;
but a woman who fears the LORD is to be praised.
Give her the reward she has earned, and let her works bring her praise at the city gate.

1. What is the value of the virtuous woman? Why?

2. Can her husband trust in her?

3. Does she help others?

4. Does she take care of her family?

5. What is her tongue like?

6. Is she busy or lazy?

7. What do her children think of her?

8. What does her husband think of her?

9. For what does she receive the most praise: charm, beauty or the fear of the Lord?

10. What speaks the loudest praise for her? (31:31)

Simple Definitions of Key Words

A	abomination	hated, horrible
	arrogant	proud, "big shot"
	attitude	how you feel about something
C	chasten	strong discipline, for example "spanking"
	commends	approves
	contention	fighting, arguing
	contrite	being sorry, repenting
D	deceit	tricks, lies
	despise	hate
	diligent	working hard, doing a good job
	discipline	teaching, training, correcting
	discretion	being careful, wise, good judgment
E	equity	fairness
	established	made firm, settled
F	favor	good feelings, approval
	flatter	praising someone too much, or
	flatter	praising someone when you don't really mean it
	forsake	give up, leave
G	generous	sharing, giving
	gossip	sharing secrets about someone else
H	hearken	hear, listen to
	humility	being humble, not proud
	hypocrite	someone who pretends to be good, but isn't
		someone who says things he doesn't mean
I	incline	turn, lean toward
	integrity	honest, true
J	judgment	deciding what's right
	just	good, fair
L	liberal	gives freely

M	mocker	scorner, ignores God's wisdom, thinks he's smart
O	oppress	push around, pick on
	oppressor	bully, mean or bossy person
P	perverse	crooked, mean, stubborn
	poverty	being poor, without money or belongings
	prosper	do well, succeed
	prudent	thinks ahead, plans carefully
R	rebuke	tell someone they are wrong
	regard	pays attention to
	reproof	correction
	reprove	tell someone they are wrong, correct them
	righteous	good person
	righteousness	doing right, being good
S	scorn	ignore
	scorner	mocker, thinks he's smart, ignores God's wisdom, rebels
	simplicity	simple ways
	slander	saying bad things about someone to hurt them , evil gossip
	sloth	fullazy
	sluggard	slow, lazy
	strife	fighting, arguing
V	void	empty
W	want	being poor, doing without
	wrath	strong anger

Verses to memorize:

Lessons 1-4

Proverbs 1:1-7 The proverbs of Solomon son of David, king of Israel: for attaining wisdom and discipline; for understanding words of insight; for acquiring a disciplined and prudent life, doing what is right and just and fair; for giving prudence to the simple, knowledge and discretion to the young— let the wise listen and add to their learning, and let the discerning get guidance— for understanding proverbs and parables, the sayings and riddles of the wise. **The fear of the LORD is the beginning of knowledge, but fools despise wisdom and discipline.**

James 3:13-17 Who is wise and understanding among you? Let him show it by his good life, by deeds done in the humility that comes from wisdom. But if you harbor bitter envy and selfish ambition in your hearts, do not boast about it or deny the truth. Such "wisdom" does not come down from heaven but is earthly, unspiritual, of the devil. For where you have envy and selfish ambition,there you find disorder and every evil practice. **But the wisdom that comes from heaven is first of all pure; then peace-loving, considerate, submissive, full of mercy and good fruit, impartial and sincere.**

Lesson 5
Proverbs 3:13 Blessed is the man who finds wisdom, the man who gains understanding,

Lesson 6
Proverbs 3:3-4 Let love and faithfulness never leave you; bind them around your neck, write them on the tablet of your heart. Then you will win favor and a good name in the sight of God and man.

Lesson 7
Proverbs 1:28-29 "Then they will call to me [wisdom] but I will not answer; they will look for me but will not find me. Since they hated knowledge and did not choose to fear the LORD.

Lesson 8
Proverbs 12:19 The truly righteous man attains life, but he who pursues evil goes to his death.

Lesson 9
Proverbs 10:11 The mouth of the righteous is a fountain of life, but violence overwhelms the mouth of the wicked.

Lesson 10
Proverbs 10:19 When words are many, sin is not absent, but he who holds his tongue is wise.

Lesson 11
Proverbs 12:18 Reckless words pierce like a sword, but the tongue of the wise brings healing..

Lesson 12
Proverbs 15:1 A gentle answer turns away wrath, but a harsh word stirs up anger.

Lesson 13
Proverbs 3:31-32 Do not envy a violent man or choose any of his ways, for the LORD detests a perverse man but takes the upright into his confidence.

Lesson 14
Proverbs 15:18 A hot-tempered man stirs up dissension, but a patient man calms a quarrel.

Lesson 15
Proverbs 22:3 A prudent man sees danger and takes refuge, but the simple keep going and suffer for it.

Lesson 16
Proverbs 3:34 He [God] mocks proud mockers but gives grace to the humble.

Lesson 17
Proverbs 1:7 The fear of the LORD is the beginning of knowledge, but fools despise wisdom and discipline.

Lesson 18
Proverbs 28:13 He who conceals his sins does not prosper, but whoever confesses and renounces them finds mercy.

Lesson 19
Proverbs 6:23 For these commands are a lamp, this teaching is a light, and the corrections of discipline are the way to life.

Lesson 20
Proverbs 16:2 All a man's ways seem innocent to him, but motives are weighed by the LORD.

Lesson 21
Proverbs 23:4 Do not wear yourself out to get rich; have the wisdom to show restraint.

Lesson 22
Proverbs 22:4 Humility and the fear of the LORD bring wealth and honor and life

Lesson 23
Proverbs 1:7 The fear of the LORD is the beginning of knowledge, but fools despise wisdom and discipline.
Proverbs 9:10 "The fear of the LORD is the beginning of wisdom, and knowledge of the Holy One is understanding.

Lesson 24
Proverbs 13:4 The sluggard craves and gets nothing, but the desires of the diligent are fully satisfied.

Passages to memorize:

Lesson 25
Proverbs 12:24 Diligent hands will rule, but laziness ends in slave labor.

Lesson 26
Proverbs 13:24 He who spares the rod hates his son, but he who loves him is careful to discipline him.

Lesson 27
Proverbs 22:24-25 Do not make friends with a hot-tempered man, do not associate with one easily angered, or you may learn his ways and get yourself ensnared.

Lesson 28
Proverbs 3:3-4 Let love and faithfulness never leave you; bind them around your neck, write them on the tablet of your heart. Then you will win favor and a good name in the sight of God and man.

Lesson 29
Proverbs 7:24-27 Now then, my sons, listen to me; pay attention to what I say. Do not let your heart turn to her ways or stray into her paths. Many are the victims she has brought down; her slain are a mighty throng. Her house is a highway to the grave, leading down to the chambers of death.

Lesson 30
Proverbs 31:30 Charm is deceptive, and beauty is fleeting; but a woman who fears the LORD is to be praised.
Proverbs 31:10 A wife of noble character who can find? She is worth far more than rubies.

CPSIA information can be obtained at www.ICGtesting.com
Printed in the USA
BVOW05s0655260713

326830BV00001B/17/P